AF255206

"In this book, Sister Maureena Fritz in her ninetieth year seeks to rethink the relationship between Judaism and Christianity. But she recognizes that this requires a new understanding of Jesus, i.e. a movement from belief in Jesus as the only way to God and salvation to an affirmation that Jesus is a way that is open to other ways. Under her skillful hands, Catholicism and Christianity are liberated to become the Gospel of Love and a worthy vehicle to bring the Kingdom of God—the goals which Jesus sought to achieve with his life. This revolution will go down in the history of all religions as one of the greatest examples of repentance and spiritual rebirth—as befits and honors a great living world religion."

—IRVING YITZ GREENBERG, SENIOR SCHOLAR IN RESIDENCE,
HADAR INSTITUTE OF NEW YORK AND JERUSALEM

"This is a book of witness. Maureena Fritz testifies to a new experience of Jesus as the revealer of a God who is an intimately loving presence to all. Only an uncompromising love of Judaism and Jews can help atone for the historical effects of the doctrine of Christian supremacy. Fritz tells us how we may begin."

—ROGER HAIGHT, SJ, VISITING PROFESSOR OF THEOLOGY,
UNION THEOLOGICAL SEMINARY

"Who better than Sr. Maureena Fritz to set about *Redeeming Jesus' Name*? Both her theology and her life are rooted in honesty, diligence, spirituality, and loyalty. This book is written by a true Jerusalemite, holding heaven and earth together in her unstinting gaze. In Hebrew we sometimes call her *Rina,* which means song. *Redeeming Jesus' Name* is Maureena's song."

—MICHAEL MARMUR, FORMER PROVOST AND ASSOCIATE
PROFESSOR OF JEWISH THEOLOGY, HEBREW UNION
COLLEGE–JEWISH INSTITUTE OF RELIGION

"Through a lifetime of witness and scholarship, Maureena Fritz has been a gift to her students, her colleagues and to the communities in which she has lived. With the same vitality she brought to seven decades of teaching and learning, she captures in this summative work the challenging appeal that Christians must humbly and critically transform the name of Jesus from obstacle to source of universal love. *Redeeming Jesus' Name* is the compelling legacy of a wise woman who knows."

—David G. Sylvester, president and vice-chancellor, University of St. Michael's College

Redeeming Jesus' Name

Redeeming Jesus' Name

*Reflections of a Ninety-Year-Old Nun
Living in Jerusalem*

MAUREENA FRITZ

Foreword by Paul F. Knitter

WIPF & STOCK · Eugene, Oregon

REDEEMING JESUS' NAME
Reflections of a Ninety-Year-Old Nun Living in Jerusalem

Wipf & Stock
An Imprint of Wipf and Stock Publishers
199 W. 8th Ave., Suite 3
Eugene, OR 97401

www.wipfandstock.com

PAPERBACK ISBN: 978-1-6667-5990-7
HARDCOVER ISBN: 978-1-6667-5991-4
EBOOK ISBN: 978-1-6667-5992-1

06/28/23
Mary Transformed, permission given by Donna M. Fyffe, President, CommunityWorks, Inc. and Deborah Asberry, Senior Consultant.

Scripture quotations are taken from the New Revised Standard Version Bible (NRSV), copyright © 1989 the Division of Christian Education of the National Council of the Churches of Christ in the United States of America. Used by permission. All rights reserved.

To

The Sisters and Brothers of Our Lady of Sion
with their unique charism to witness in the church God's
faithful love for the Jewish people

and

The Worldwide Association of Bat Kol Alumni

Contents

Foreword

A MORE FITTING SUBTITLE of this book might be "An *Appeal* of a Ninety-Year-Old Nun Living in Jerusalem." What Sister Maureena Fritz offers in this book are more than "reflections." What one hears in these pages is an appeal, indeed, a cri de coeur.

It is a heart-cry to her fellow Christians to do what they should have done centuries ago, especially since the horrors of the Holocaust: to redeem the name of Jesus from the way it has been used to ground or justify anti-Semitism.

This appeal comes from the heart of a woman who has spent eighty years of her life as a Sister of Sion—a religious order that defines its mission as "to witness in the Church God's faithful love for the Jewish people" and "to build bridges between the Jews and the Church—without proselytizing." She has lived in Jerusalem for the past thirty years, and, in 1992, she became an Israeli citizen.

A "cri de coeur," as Webster's defines it, is a passionate outcry.[1] Sr. Maureena's outcry is indeed passionate. But it is also courageous. Maybe it's the courage that comes with age when one feels that time is running out; maybe it's the courage born of her many pointed, pained conversations with Holocaust survivors and her fellow Israeli citizens.

Whatever the source of her courage, I have found few Christian theologians who have dared to so clearly recognize and then to so penitently confess that the anti-Semitism that has infected so much of Western history (Europe and the Americas) has been

---

1. "Cri de coeur," Merriam-Webster.

justified, even motivated, by what Christians, throughout church history, have believed and taught about the Jews.

With scholarly precision, Sr. Maureena lays bare how the roots of the anti-Semitism that showed its full face in the Holocaust and that still persists in multifarious forms are to be found in the New Testament itself and in the long and still standing Christian theology of what scholars call "supersessionism"—or in ordinary parlance: Christian supremacy.

She recognizes the recent and sincere efforts of the Catholic Church within and since the Second Vatican Council to admit and address the "contempt" that has stained Christian attitudes and vitiated Christian conduct toward Jews. But she also identifies what most theologians don't, or don't want to, recognize: that the many recent Vatican statements that call for better relations and dialogue with Jews are interwoven with traditional references to Jesus as the one and only savior and Son of God and to the church as the new covenant or the new Israel.

All such language, she reminds the overseers of the Magisterium, necessarily imply that the *new* covenant is intended by God to fulfill and complete the *old*. "Fulfillment," she notes, is dangerously close to "replacement."

She offers a recent and telling example of how this reluctance, or inability, to critically reexamine such traditional claims about Jesus and the church can infect even the most sincere attempts to achieve more respectful and mutual relations of the church with Jews. In August of 2021, she reminds us, Pope Francis, in a heartfelt expression of goodwill and brotherly love toward Jews, ended his invitation with a reference to St. Paul's letters and a reminder that "those who seek life need to look to the promise and to its fulfillment in Christ."[2]

Here Sr. Maureena's heart-born appeal becomes a sobering challenge: Unless sincere Christians, like Pope Francis, are able to recognize, and then remedy, the way their traditional language about Jesus as the "only Son of God" and the "only way to the Father" has led, willy-nilly and often contrary to their intentions, to

2. See page 91 of this book.

claims of Christian superiority and supremacy over Judaism and all other religions, they will not be able to "redeem the name of Jesus."

Few contemporary Christian theologians have sounded this challenge with such clarity, coherence, and urgency.

But she not only sounds this challenge; she also offers guidance on how to respond to it. In the opening chapters of her book she lays out and then adopts the lessons Christians can learn from "Jewish hermeneutics"—the way Jews have preserved and interpreted God's revelation in past history and the written word. The Torah, Jewish teachers announce, is not a fixed, permanent treasure to be protected and passed on through the generations; rather, it is like wheat from which to make flour, or like flax to fashion ever new garments, or like granite from which to carve abundant sculptures.

And this ongoing process of interpreting—of baking and sewing and carving—must be carried on in community, through multiple voices that form a chorus and sometimes a cacophony, and in which no one voice can be held up as solely true and final.

Sr. Maureena calls Christians to take up the task of making new flour, new garments, new images in interpreting how Christians are to understand and follow the person and message of Jesus the Christ. And she offers her own effort to do so—to carry on this task of interpreting the witness of the New Testament and of trying, once again, to answer Jesus' question: "Who do you say I am?"

Her leitmotif in this interpretative task is to rediscover and reassess *the Jewishness of Jesus*. She makes clear that if we truly understand that Jesus, from his early years to his death on the cross, was a faithful Jew, that as a Jew he was indeed a son of God and as a Jewish prophet he was as critical of his religion as he was faithful to it, then the idea of forming a new movement or religion in opposition to or replacement of his Jewish tradition would have been for him inconceivable. Such "parting of the ways" in which his followers saw themselves in opposition to Judaism would come later.

But Sr. Maureena makes clear that to reaffirm the Jewishness of Jesus can enable us not to reject but to reappropriate the later Christian claims of his divinity and of his saving message. Jesus remains "the way to the God who is Father/Mother," but he is "a way that is open to other ways."

In giving voice to her "appeal" and to her "cri de coeur," this book stands, I believe, as a kind of last will and testament—her major, perhaps final, effort, as a good Sister of Sion, to call her church to recognize "God's faithful love for the Jewish people" but also to recognize that such a faithful love rules out all traditional assertions of Christian supremacy.

May her voice be heard and her legacy live on.

PAUL F. KNITTER, Paul Tillich Emeritus Professor of Theology and Religions, Union Theological Seminary, New York City

Preface

Jesus weeping: *Jesus and the Last Apostle*, by Reuven Ruben, 1922

THIS BOOK IS ADDRESSED to all those who honor Jesus and also to all those who have been persecuted in his name.

Christians who have taken the words in John's Gospel (14:6) literally and believe that Jesus is the only way to the Father have dishonored Jesus' name. In this book I propose an understanding of Jesus as a way that is open to other ways.

In dealing with this topic, certain images stand out in my mind. In this painting, *Jesus and the Last Apostle*, by Reuven Ruben, the wounded Jesus is sitting on the left weeping over all the Jews who have been persecuted for not accepting him as their Messiah. Galla Galaction, a staunch opponent of anti-Semitism in Romania, weeps with him.

My first personal encounter with Jews occurred on my post-doctoral sabbatical in Israel, while doing research on the historical Jesus. The many Holocaust survivors whom I met provided me with a faith-shaking experience. Most of them told me how numerous Christians supported the Nazis in their persecution of the Jews. I found it hard to believe them, yet it was a blessing—it led me to study the history of the church with the Jewish people. Totally shocking. I was horrified at what I learned. What the Nazis did, except for liquidation of the Jews, was paralleled in the history of the church. Christianity defined itself by its hostility toward Jews and Judaism.

Ecclesia and Synagoga, unknown artist, c. 1230

Anti-Judaism is embodied in these two sculptures in the cathedral in Strasbourg (1230 CE); the church triumphant replaces Israel, the defeated woman, whose head is bowed, her staff broken, her eyes blindfolded, and the Torah slipping from her hands.

The same theology continues to lurk in recent official teachings of the Catholic Church. In *Nostra Aetate*, the Second Vatican Council's *Declaration of the Relation of the Church to Non-Christian Religions*, it is stated, "As Holy Scripture testifies, Jerusalem did not recognize the time of her visitation."[1] In its 1975 *Guidelines* for interpreting *Nostra Aetate*, the Vatican expressly declares that Jesus is "the fulfillment and perfection of the earlier Revelation."[2] Applying this to the church, the Vatican in 1985 declares that the mission of the church is to be "the all-embracing means of salvation" in which alone "the fullness of the means of salvation can be obtained."[3] Even more disparagingly, in 2002, in its statement on *The Jewish People*, the Vatican declares that Jews find themselves in a situation of disobedience to God for their refusal of faith in Christ.[4]

My first two chapters are tools to help Christians move from belief in Jesus as the only way to the Father to an affirmation of Jesus as a way that is open to other ways. Chapter 1 is on interpretation of Scripture—the word of God in Scripture is not frozen but open to multiple interpretations that can be correlated with ongoing experience. Chapter 2 is an analysis of how God spoke to different personalities in the Hebrew Scriptures and continues to speak to us today.

In chapters 3 and 4, I demonstrate the consequences of a literal translation of "No one comes to the Father except through me" (John 14:6). Chapter 3 is a summary of the history of the church with the Jewish people. Chapter 4 is on replacement theology. In chapter 5 I deal with a central issue in Christology: "Did the first

---

1. Vatican Commission, *Guidelines*, sect. 4; Paul VI, *Declaration on the Relation*.

2. Vatican Commission, *Guidelines*, sect. 3.

3. Vatican Commission, *Notes*, sect. 1.

4. Pontifical Biblical Commission, *Jewish People*, sect. 42.

Christians worship Jesus?" The last two chapters are personal. In chapter 6, I focus on who is Jesus for me—a way open to other ways. I conclude in chapter 7 with my reflections on who is God for me—God who defies definition but is open to many descriptions.

The Epilogue emphasizes the need to move from a traditional stance of "superiority over" to one of "authentic dialogue with" Judaism and other religions. This will require a pluralistic Christology that renews Jesus' focus on the reign of God rather than the reign of the church and that understands Jesus as "a way that is open to other ways."

A Personal Introduction

"Redeeming Jesus' Name"

—Maureena Fritz

When I sent my book, entitled *Redeeming Jesus' Name*, to Wipf and Stock publishers on March 19, 2023, two nagging questions unsettled my joy: Should I have asked the sensitive questions I asked, and should I publish the controversial answers I found to some of my questions? Two closely related events gave me the answers I was looking for.

The first episode was the online celebration of the fortieth anniversary of the foundation of the Bat Kol Institute on February 27, 2023. During the celebration, Rabbi Weiman-Kelman spoke of the fragments of the broken tablets (Exod 32:15, 19). He said that each fragment represented a small piece of truth, which each of us holds; no one can claim access to absolute truth.

The second episode occurred while I was reading a commentary on the Passover haggadah. The haggadah tells of four sons: first the wise son, then the wicked son, followed by the simple son, and, finally, the son who doesn't know to ask. Elie Wiesel described the four sons and their attitude to asking questions: that of the wise son, who knows the question and asks it; that of the wicked son, who knows the question but refuses to ask it; that of the simple son, who knows the question but is indifferent to it; and finally, that of the ignorant son, who does not know the question and therefore is unable to ask.[1]

The answers I received from these two episodes silenced my anxiety. In asking questions, I was in the company of the wise son who dared to ask difficult questions. My fragments of truth placed side by side with the fragments of truths of others will lead to a fuller truth.

I've struggled long in the writing of this book. As its birthday approaches in about six months, my hope is that the questions I've asked and the answers I've proposed will evoke further discussion of questions that we cannot hide from.

---

1. Wiesel. Passover Haggadah, 6.

Acknowledgments

My special appreciation goes to Paul Knitter for our never-ending discussions on the issues at hand and for his continuous intellectual probing. He read all the sections in progress and gifted me with his telling questions and suggestions.

I am also deeply grateful to my fellow Sisters of Our Lady of Sion for their continual interest in this book and their encouragement to proceed in the face of the sensitive issues that it takes up.

My research was greatly enhanced through my encounter with the various theologies of Bat Kol alums living across the seven continents. And, last but not least, what I have written is my limited but I hope helpful response to the challenging questions of survivors of the Holocaust and of my Israeli fellow citizens.

Special thanks go to editors at Wipf and Stock Publishers, Elisabeth Richard and Savanah N. Landerholm. I deeply appreciate their gracious and immediate replies to every question and concern I raised.

Chapter 1

Interpretation: God's Word Is Not Frozen in the Past

The path to theology . . . is grounded in the forms of experience found in the natural world. In the course of time, these forms and their linguistic expressions weave a web of habitude; the raw and the real are stifled by routine. There is much to do one thinks and it is good to work in a settled sphere with established patterns. But the fissures happen in any case, and in unexpected ways; and the human being is awakened, if only for the time being, to vaster dimensions of experience and the contingencies of existence.

–Michael Fishbane[1]

____

1. Fishbane, *Sacred Attunement*, x.

A lesson in chanting the Torah

As I've already stated, this book is my attempt to redeem Jesus' name from the sinful way in which his name has been used by so many of his followers to demean and replace Jews. And in order to do that, I'm going to have to deal with the way the sacred texts of Christianity have presented Jesus Christ and the church that followed him as the fulfillment and then the replacement of the Jewish religion.

In other words, I'm going to have to take up the complex task of *reinterpreting* traditional ways of understanding the foundational text of Christianity—the New Testament. I have to do that, because if these interpretations of the New Testament are correct, then I would have to be honest with myself and admit that I could no longer be a Christian. *Reinterpretation* is for me, and I know for many Christians, a faith-saving, life-saving task.

And to carry out that task, I have been immensely helped by the very Jewish tradition that I am trying to respect and cherish— the Talmudic method of interpreting the Bible.

TALMUDIC RABBINIC METHODS OF INTERPRETATION

The most helpful thing I learned from studying the Talmudic method of interpretation was that it allows for a "this" and a "that"; that is, opposing interpretations. This led me to realize that by dialoguing with those who hold opposing views, I discover the truth, and I learn that there can be multiple and even different interpretations of a particular text of the Bible.

> When two Babylonian sages disagree with each other about the law there is no untruth there. Each of them justifies his opinion. One gives a reason to permit, the other reason to forbid. One compares the case before him to one precedent; the other compares it to something different. It is possible to say, "both speak the words of the living God." At times, one reason is valid; at other times, another reason. For reasons change in the wake of even only small alternatives.[2]

God's revelation to Moses at Sinai is central to both Jews and Christians. The biblical account of this revelation—an account of the covenant of promises and responsibilities, enacted between God and the Israelite people—is a foundational event for the Jewish people.[3] The covenant was sealed with the response of the people, "We will hear and we will do" (Deut 5:27).

The rabbis returned again and again to this focusing event, and they asked themselves: Was the fullness of divine revelation given at Sinai or does God continue to reveal the divine Self? That is, is God's revelation simply a matter of transmission of what was revealed at Sinai? as indicated in the *Pirke Avoth*, which tells us, "Moses received the Torah on Sinai, and handed it down to Joshua; Joshua to the elders; the elders to the prophets; and the prophets handed it down to the men of the great assembly."[4]

2. Rashi, *Ketuvot*, 57a.

3. Kessler, "Jewish Response," 158

4. Pirkei Avot, 1:1.

A text in the book of Numbers suggests that teaching is not simply "a passing on" but a process of interpretation that is influenced by the changing conditions of life.

> So, the LORD said to Moses, "Gather for me seventy of the elders of Israel, whom you know to be the elders of the people and officers over them; bring them to the tent of meeting, and have them take their place there with you. I will come down and talk with you there; and I will take some of the spirit that is on you and put it on them. (Num 11:6–17)

Though it is a process of interpretation, interpretation is not divorced from the revelation at Sinai. The teaching of the scribes is said to be contained in the revelation to Moses at Sinai but not in frozen form: "The Holy One, blessed be God, gave the Torah to Israel as wheat from which to make fine flour, and as flax from which to make a garment."[5]

Encounter with a rock and encounter with the Torah have similar characteristics. Michelangelo spent hours before a rock before he sculpted *David*. Interpreters of Scripture spend hours before a biblical text. Two processes are employed: exegesis and eisegesis. Exegesis is unearthing what is in the text. This is considered to be an objective approach to the text and is known as the *peshat* level. *Peshat* stands for the plain literal meaning of the text. Eisegesis is what the interpreter brings to the text and reads into the text from one's personal experience, which leads into three other kinds of interpretation: *remez* (hint), *midrash* (homiletic) and *sod* (secret).

From this we learn that teaching the biblical message is not just a matter of transmission—it is a matter of interpretation, which is deeply affected by the challenges of life. Interpretations of Scripture are not fixed in the past: "Ultimately the real source and stimulus for a vital orientation to life had to be the environment and the novel challenges which each day produced."[6]

Michael Fishbane asks,

5. *Tanna Devei Eliyahu* 2:1.

6. Cohen, *Talmudic Age*, 175.

> And insofar as we are heirs to religious formulations from the past, sometimes centuries and millennia removed from our present circumstances, with their often vastly different intellectual ideals and challenges, it is also necessary to ask, in what way is the language of scripture real or true or compelling for us, given its personalized portrayals of God and divine dominion, or its particular picture of the world order and its spiritual entities? How do they jibe with our contemporary sense of language and spirituality and cosmos? . . . in what respect (if at all) is the language of the ancient rabbis a living truth or instructions for us today, saturated as it is with age-specific personifications of God and the divine universe as a whole?[7]

We must therefore have the courage to question our beliefs:

> Traditions mask our thoughts, and glib pieties provide the hiding places where we crouch against the thunderous question: Where are you—just now in your life? We must therefore have the courage to examine our beliefs (both received and constructed) and determine what is intellectually or spiritually viable. No evasions should be permitted as we each ask, in what sense is God a living reality in our lives, or merely some abstraction of thought; and in what respect is religious life a matter of true engagement, or simply an expression of inherited behaviors?[8]

One of the main intents of Michael Fishbane is to save "the study of scripture from being a merely historical retrieval of information, and the history of interpretation from becoming an archive of achievements."[9]

Jewish biblical interpreters recognize that God spoke once upon a time to Israel at Mount Sinai, but those were not God's final words. As God continued to speak to Israel through the events of life, the words of the written torah were significantly expanded and

7. Fishbane, *Sacred Atunement*, 2.

8. Fishbane, *Sacred Atunement*, 2.

9. Fishbane, *Sacred Atunement*, xi.

transformed by the pulse of ongoing life, generation after generation as the disciples of Moses investigated what was inscribed and needed interpretation, and as they expanded the original norms through faithful living and ancestral practice. Over time, the breath of the oral torah suffused the ancient text and inspired it with new soul and sanctity, extending the path of piety outlined in the initial covenant to the emergent patterns and particulars of everyday life.[10]

I ask whether there is a contradiction between God's revelation in the Bible and what we know to be true in our daily lives. If there is, which has the final authority over us: Scripture or own experience? My answer, based on my own life experience and study of Jewish hermeneutics: Neither! Neither the Bible nor my own human experience has a pre-given, absolute authority. Scripture and human experiences must remain in dialogue with one another. The written text is significantly expanded and transformed by our experience of life and the findings of science. And our ongoing human condition continues to be challenged and clarified by the written word of God. We keep ourselves rooted in God's past revelations to humankind: "Your word is a lamp to my feet and a light to my path" (Ps 119:105).

CHRISTIAN INTERPRETATION OF SCRIPTURE

John Henry Newman, a Christian theologian (b. 1801) describes a university as a place for the education of the intellect to discriminate between truth and falsehood, for sifting out the grains of truth from the mass, and arranging things according to their real value.

> Truth of whatever kind is the proper object of the intellect; its cultivation then lies in fitting it to apprehend and contemplate truth. . .We know, not by a direct and simple vision, not at a glance, but, as it were, by piecemeal and accumulation, by a mental process, by going round an object, by the comparison, the combination, the mutual correction, the continual adaptation, of many partial

10. Fishbane, *Sacred Atunement*, 114–15

> notions, by the employment, concentration, and joint
> action of many faculties and exercises of mind.[11]

According to Newman, Catholic education and theology are not unlike Talmudic rabbinic understanding of interpretation; they are thus much more than a simple acceptance of the doctrines and teachings of the church, a diet upon which I was first educated. Newman's method of pursuing the truth "by piecemeal and accumulation . . . by the comparison, the combination . . . the continual adaptation of many partial notions" resonates with what Paul Tillich described as the "method of correlation" for Christian theologians[12]—a method that itself resonates with rabbinic interpretation.

Both Jewish and Christian theologians stress that God's revelation is continuing. Past interpretations, as Tillich proposed, must be correlated with ongoing experience, with what the movement of history, science, the arts tells us about the human condition. New discoveries and new happenings bring new questions. We explore these new questions in the light of the scriptures, and we explore the biblical witness in the light of our new questions. Christian theology and self-understanding are an ongoing, mutually clarifying and mutually criticizing dialogue between what we believe has been revealed to us in the past and what we are struggling with in the present.[13]

These Talmudic and Christian understandings of interpretation give Christians the permission to question all aspects of their faith. Many of the church's dogmas and teachings are frozen in absolutist formulations. Catholic theology before the sixties was definitely not following a method of correlation. Vatican II partially changed that. It opened the windows and let in warm winds that began a melting process on different topics. An example of the church's new understanding of itself is contained in article 8 of *Lumen Gentium*. Before Vatican II it was stated that the true

---

11. Newman, "Discourse 7."

12. Tillich, *Systematic Theology*, 1:64–66.

13. See Hill et al., *Faith, Religion, and Theology*, 285–301.

church of Christ *is* the Roman Catholic Church. The Council Fathers changed the little word "is" (*est*) to "exists in" (*subsistit in*). From an exclusive understanding of itself as the one true church of Christ, it recognized that the true church of Christ could also exist in other denominations. Another example of a quite revolutionary shift in church doctrine came in Vatican II's *Nostra Aetate*. After more than two thousand years of understanding itself as the new Israel of God, the church implicitly but clearly recognized the Jewish people as a people in continuing covenant with God and not superseded by the church.

INFALLIBILITY AND THE METHOD OF CORRELATION

But while there are striking similarities between the talmudic-rabbinic method of interpretation and much of Catholic-Christian theology, there are also striking differences. And here is where much can be, and needs to be, learned by Christians. One of the most evident differences is that for Jewish interpreters, there never is, and there never can be, only one exclusive, or one final, interpretation. The richness of God's Truth can never be captured in "only one" or in a "once and for all" understanding. In human terms, God's truth—or humans' understanding of God's truth—will always be many. It can never be only one. Truth, if it is God's truth, will always be "on its way," always in process of being understood. And it will include, or make room for, other truths rather than excluding them.

To understand God's truth as always being "many truths" does not mean, however, that God's truth is "any truth." I am not talking about rampant relativism where anything goes. Visit any yeshiva and see and hear what I'm getting at. Yeshivas are noisy because people are arguing for the truth. Different students are taking strong, vocal stands on what they believe to be a correct interpretation of a particular text. But they are doing so in conversation with others who have other interpretations, often contradictory interpretations. Here is the beauty, the mystery, and the challenge of the talmudic method: Other interpretations, even when they are contradictory, are not excluded. In their differences, in their contradictoriness, they are not just allowed; they are needed. They have to be part of the conversation. Even when I disagree with you, I am affirming you because I have to continue talking with you if I am going to properly understand and live by what I believe to be true. This is the definition of authentic dialogue. One affirms one's truth clearly and firmly, but never absolutely, never conclusively, never exclusively.

Chapter 2

God Speaks to Us in the Events of Our Lives

WE WILL HEAR AND WE WILL DO (DEUT 5:27)

The relation of faith is no book of rules which can be looked up to discover what is to be done now, in this very hour. I experience what God desires of me for this hour—so far as I do experience it—not earlier. . . . Only one thing matters, that as the situation is presented to me, I expose myself to it as to the word's manifestation to me, to the very ground where hearing passes into being.

–MARTIN BUBER[1]

TWO OF MY MOST favored lines in the Bible are the words, "We will hear and we will do" (Deut 5:27) and its companion, *We will do and we will hear* (Exod 24:3–7, emphasis mine). Hearing leads to doing and doing sharpens hearing.

1. Buber, *Between Man and Man*, 68, 69.

When I studied the history of the church with the Jewish people, I felt that God was talking to me. I became convinced that this history laid a foundation for the Nazi extermination of over six million Jews in incinerators across Europe. My faith, as a Christian, was sorely tested. I became convinced that if we, as a church, ignore this tragedy, all our assertions about Jesus are empty.

When I say ignore, I mean to ignore God speaking to us through this tragedy. And when I say "to us," I have to ask where am I in this "us"? I must make efforts to hear God speaking to me.

But how do I hear God's voice? How does God reveal the divine Self to me? When I entered the convent, as an eighteen-year-old, I felt that God was calling me. After I arrived, I didn't hear much talk about God speaking personally to anyone. The voice of my superiors, of our Rule, and teachings from the Vatican became the vehicles though which I was to hear God's voice. Obedience to these voices ruled the day. For years I lived a life that I can describe as "stimulus-response"; that is, when the bell rang for prayer, I dropped everything and went to chapel, as one of Pavlov's dogs would have done.

At that time, I accepted what the church taught, though I was often disturbed. A secret anger burned inside me, when, as a member of a highly educated community of nuns, I sat with them listening to a young, inexperienced priest just out of seminary, or an older priest who hadn't read a theology book since ordination, preach to us at Mass on how to live our religious lives. Why could not one of us be the celebrant at the Mass!

But thank God, I was given an opportunity to pursue theological studies. During this time my whole concept of religion changed. Religion was more than truths to be believed, rites to be performed, and laws to be observed.

I felt deeply that God had indeed guided me into the convent and that God continued to lead me. But at the same time, questions persisted: If God "speaks," how does that happen? Through direct communication? Or indirectly, through an intermediary, a go-between, such as popes, bishops, superiors? Is Jesus the only way to God (John 1:6)?

I found an answer to this question as I wrote my doctoral thesis on revelation.[2] The answer is summed up in Deut 6:5: "You shall love the LORD your God with all your heart, and with all your soul, and with all your might." The command is given directly to the "you" in the singular.

But where to find God's dwelling place! In the heavens above human reach, or present among us? Members of all religions have experienced God or Ultimate Reality as present. Rabbi Ishmael Joseph Soloveitchik, a Jewish scholar born in Russia in 1903, wrote,

> The Jews gave G-d the remarkable attribute of *makom* (place). The Lord is envisaged as the *Mekomo shel olam*, the repository of the universe. What is this attribute of "place" for a G-d Who is infinite and omnipresent? By intuiting the attribute of *makom* the Halacha (Law) revealed to the world a revolutionary concept of God. He is not transcendent, mysterious, and inapproachable, but our immediate Companion. We live in G-d and experience Him in His full immediacy.[3]

And Martin Buber, a Jewish philosopher, wrote,

> One should beware altogether of understanding the conversation with God . . . as something that occurs merely apart from or above the everyday. God's address to (us) penetrates the events in all our lives and all the events in the world around us, everything biographical and everything historical, and turns it into instruction, into demands for you and me.[4]

With thoughts of this kind in mind, I begin this chapter with the question, How does God speak to us? To answer this question, I focus on a number of biblical figures: How did God speak to Eve, to Abraham, to the four women in the genealogy of Jesus in Matthew's Gospel (Tamar, Rahab, Ruth, Bathsheba) and to Moses? My reason for choosing these women was the questionability of their lives.

---

2. Fritz, *Revelation and Self Understanding*.

3. Soloveitchik, "Sacred and Profane," 63.

4. Buber, *I and Thou*, 182.

My hope is that in looking more deeply into these stories of how God spoke to these biblical characters in the situations of their lives, I may better understand how God is speaking to the church and to me today on a special subject, the Holocaust. Strange as this may seem, Jesus' name is connected to the Holocaust because of the way the church, down through the ages, pitted Jesus against the Jews, a topic I will examine in forthcoming pages.

EVE: THE MOTHER OF LIFE (GEN 2:4—3:24)

Adam and Eve: *Adam & Eve,* by Gustave Dore, 1877

First, I ask, How does one judge whether interpretations are life-giving or death-dealing? I find the answer in Matthew's Gospel where Jesus says, "Thus you will know them by their fruits" (Matt 7:20).

In the second story of creation (Gen 2:4—3:24), God created Adam and Eve and put them into the garden of Eden. God said to Adam, "You may freely eat of every tree of the garden; but of the tree of the knowledge of good and evil you shall not eat, for in the day that you eat of it you shall die." A serpent in the garden appeared to Eve and said, "You will not die; for God knows that when you eat of it your eyes will be opened, and you will be like God, knowing good and evil." So she ate of the fruit and gave some to her husband to eat. He too ate of the fruit. They were cast out of the garden, Eve to bring forth children in pain and Adam to earn his living by the sweat of his brow. The serpent was condemned to crawl on his belly and eat dust all the days of his life.

Interpretations of this story condemned women and honored men:

> From a woman was sin's beginning, and because of her, we all die. (Sir 25:24)

> In such a form he (the devil) entered paradise and corrupted Eve. But he did not contact Adam. (2 Enoch 31:4–6)

> Adam said to Eve, "Why have you brought destruction among us and brought upon us great wrath, which is death gaining rule over all our race?" (Apocalypse of Moses 2:17)

> For God created man for incorruption (immortality), and made him in the image of his own eternity, but through the devil's envy death entered the world. (Wis 1:13; 2:23–24)

We now know that the creation stories are mythical accounts of creation that attempt to explain suffering, death, and evil. Certain interpretations, with time, become part of the myth and become so solidly embedded in the human psyche that they are almost impossible to uproot. Such has happened with the story of creation.

In the account of creation, there is no mention of Satan. The serpent is not Satan. The serpent is the "shrewdest of all the wild beasts that the Lord God had made" (Gen 3:1). Animals were credited with speaking with a human voice: "It is said that in olden times . . . snakes could speak with a man's voice."[5]

The serpent opened the conversation with the woman by asking, "Did God really say, 'You shall not eat of any tree of the garden'?" Eve replied, "We may eat of the fruit of the trees in the garden; but God said, 'You shall not eat of the fruit of the tree that is in the middle of the garden, nor shall you touch it, or you shall die'" (Gen 3:3).

The serpent replied, "You will not die; for God knows that when you eat of it your eyes will be opened, and you will be like God, knowing good and evil."

Eve looked at the tree, saw that it was good for food, a delight to the eyes, and to be desired to make one wise. She said to herself, "All the things that my husband told me are lies." And so, she decided to take a bite.[6] And lo and behold, all that the serpent told her came true! Adam and Eve didn't die, at least not right away; Adam lived to the age of 930 (Gen 5:5). Not only did they not die, but as the serpent promised, they became like God. And God said, "See, the man has become like one of us, knowing good and evil" (Gen 3:22).

Adam and Eve had come of age (Gen 3:23). No need existed for them to remain in the garden of Eden as pampered children. So God banished them from the nursery to till the soil from which they had been taken. To prevent any return, God locked the doors to Eden (Gen 3:24).

Out in the world, Adam and Eve assumed their responsibility to care for the earth, yes with suffering and pain, but with the joy of becoming co-creators with God.

"The man named his wife Eve, because she was the mother of all living" (Gen 3:20). Eve, *chavah* in Hebrew, is a name that refers to *chavah*, to breathe, and *chayah*, to live or to give life. The biblical text defines Eve as "the mother of all the living."[7]

---

5. Philo, *On the Creation*, 156.

6. Avot de Rabbi Natan, ch. 1.

7. Kugel, *Bible as It Was*, 65–82.

To Conclude

Eve is the model I set up for women. She took her own life into her hands and made her own decisions. She knew that God had told Adam not to eat the fruit of the tree of the knowledge of good and evil and that if he did, he would die. But as she listened to the serpent, her eyes were opened. She found the serpent's words convincing. She ate the fruit. She didn't die. She became like God knowing good and evil. She was thrown out of the garden. Yes, she would suffer, but that was the price of independence.

THE CALL OF ABRAHAM

> Now the LORD said to Abram, "Go from your country and your kindred and your father's house to the land that I will show you. I will make of you a great nation, and I will bless you, and make your name great, so that you will be a blessing. I will bless those who bless you . . . and in you all the families of the earth shall be blessed." (Gen 12:1–3)

What a surprising introduction! Who is Abram? Up to this point readers are given but a scant introduction to Abraham (Gen 11:26–31). Here he steps unto the biblical stage as the specially chosen one of God. What had he done to be promised that he would become the ancestor of a great and mighty nation in whom all the families of the earth would be blessed? And how did God talk to him? That is my most intriguing question.

We are not given answers to these questions in the Genesis text. If we rely only on the biblical text, it seems that he had done nothing. Interpreters of the text were not satisfied with such an answer, so they went looking for other texts in Scripture for enlightenment. A door was opened for them in Josh 24:2–3:

> And Joshua said to all the people, "Thus says the LORD, the God of Israel: Long ago your ancestors—Terah and his sons Abraham and Nahor—lived beyond the Euphrates and served other gods. Then I took your father

> Abraham from beyond the River and led him through all the land of Canaan and made his offspring many. I gave him Isaac.

According to this text, Abraham and his family were idol worshipers living in Haran. Abram was the son of Terah. Life changed for Abraham when he began to question his cultural heritage. He wandered around in his mind seeking for answers. Maimonides wrote,

> When this giant was weaned he began to roam around in his mind, while he was still small, and began to think by day and by night, and he would wonder, "How is it possible that this sphere moves constantly without there being a mover, or one to turn it, for it is impossible that it turns itself?" . . . his parents and the whole people worshipped idols and he worshipped with them. But his mind roamed in search of understanding till he achieved the true way . . . he knew that there is one God who moves the spheres, who created everything, and there is none beside him. . . . Abraham was forty years old when he recognized his Creator.[8]

Through constant turmoil and questioning Abraham came to believe in God. He was forty then. Now he is seventy-five when he hears God tell him to leave his home and his country and go to a land "that I will show you." What brought this about?

Rashi (1040–1105), a renowned medieval French commentator on the Bible and the Talmud, wrote, "The meaning of the command, *lekh lekha*, go forth (Gen 12:1), is 'Go forth for your own good.'"[9] It was a deep feeling Abram had within himself. He had to leave. He had to go somewhere else.

Zornberg emphasized that what Abram felt was not just a human drive within him that pushed him to act—it was a divine-human urge "mysteriously originating within Abram himself for the sake of his own enlargement and self-realization."[10]

8. Maimonides, *Avodah Zarah*, 1:3.

9. Rashi on Gen 12:1.

10. Zornberg, *Genesis*, 79.

He must leave. But what went wrong that "he must leave for his own good"? Zornberg focuses on the phrase, "She had no child" (Gen 11:30). These three Hebrew words, *ein la vlad*, are key. Abraham's life was barren, his wife was barren, his family who were idol worshipers were barren. Deep feelings of dissatisfaction overcame him. He had to do something. He couldn't continue living with a barren wife in a barren landscape. Dissatisfied, he left.

That is how God talked to him—through his dissatisfaction. Zornberg wrote, "Every human action has its starting point in a dissatisfaction."[11] *Lech lecha*, go for your own good. "Go from your country and your kindred and your father's house to the land that I will show you" (Gen 12:1). As you walk, you will reach *"the land that I will show you."*

But the journey was terrible:

> "To the land that I will show you": He wandered aimlessly from nation to nation and kingdom to kingdom, till he reached Canaan, when God told him, "to your seed I shall give this land" (Gen 2:7). This was the fulfillment of "to the land that I will show you," and therefore he settled there . . . Before that, he did not yet know that that land was the subject of the command . . . that is why he later said to Abimelekh, "God made me wander from my father's house" (Gen 20:13). For indeed, he wandered like a lost lamb.[12]

And how did he know he had arrived in Canaan? It felt right. He sensed God saying to him, "To your seed I shall give this land."

To Conclude

God was with Abraham even when he was worshiping other gods. A divine-human drive within him drove him to ask questions. The more questions he asked, the more uncomfortable he became with his life. He reached the point of total dissatisfaction and knew he had to leave home and country. God was with him in his

11. Zornberg, *Genesis*, 73–74.

12. Zornberg, *Genesis*, 75.

dissatisfaction, perhaps even increasing it, until he could no longer continue living his life as he was living it. The moment came when he heard "*Lech lecha*," "Go from your country and your kindred and your father's house to the land that I will show you."

He was probably highly disturbed. The moment had come to make a major decision. Should I go or shouldn't I go? If I go, where will I go? He took the step. He dared to do what he felt he must do. He set out "to go to a land that I will show you."

Acting on these divine-human urges may come at great cost. Eve was thrown out of the garden of Eden to survive on her own resources. Abraham entered a wilderness not knowing his destination.

Acting on divine-human urges occurs in the present, in the taking of what seems to be the next right step. But what does one do when there is seemingly no right step, when all the options are negative? That is my next topic as I reflect on the life of Tamar.

TAMAR: SHE SIMPLY KNEW

Only those who attempt the absurd can achieve the impossible.

—Albert Einstein

"We will hear and we will do" (Deut 5:27). Such an announcement must be fulfilled by taking the next right step. But what if there is no right step? Is one freed from making a choice? Some say that not to choose is worse than making a flawed choice. To cast some light on this question I am going to take four biblical women mentioned in Matthew's genealogy, Tamar, Rahab, Ruth, and Bathsheba, and let them speak for themselves.

Tamar Speaks (Gen 38)

"Judah, the fourth son of the patriarch Jacob and Leah, his concubine, had three sons: Er, Onan and Shelah. Judah gave me as wife to Er. But he died. Then Judah gave me as wife to Onan in order to raise up seed to Er, but he died before a son was born. Then Judah promised that when his son Shelah had grown up he would arrange our marriage. But it didn't happen. Shelah had grown to manhood, yet Judah, my father-in-law, did not give him to me in marriage, as he promised. Many of my neighbors were whispering that I had a demon because my two former husbands, Er and Onan, died suddenly. And some of my neighbors looked upon me with disdain because I didn't know who my parents were.

"I anguished over this. I had a serious responsibility to raise up offspring to Judah and I was getting older and older. Then one day Bath-Shuah (1 Chr 2:4), the Canaanite wife of my father-in-law, Judah, died. After his time of mourning, I heard that he was going up to Timnah to shear his sheep (Gen 38:13–14). Should I, or shouldn't I? I asked myself. There and then I put off my widow's clothes, put on a veil, wrapped myself up, and sat down at a place on the road to Timnah. Don't think I felt brave. My heart was pounding with fear. I could be killed for what I was going to do.

"As I sat there trembling, I saw my father-in-law approaching. He saw me and didn't recognize me and he said, 'Come, let me come in to you.' I said, 'What will you give me, that you may come in to me?' He answered, 'I will send you a kid from the flock.' I replied, 'Only if you give me a pledge, until you send it.' He said, 'What pledge shall I give you?' I said, 'Your signet and your cord, and the staff that is in your hand.' He gave them to me and came in unto me. Afterwards, we both went on our way.

"It wasn't long before I knew I was pregnant. While I was joyful, I was also terrified. As I was getting bigger, I thought of disappearing, but I knew that would defeat my purpose. My father-in-law would have to know. And so it happened. My father-in-law heard about my illegitimate pregnancy and he said, 'Bring her out, and let her be burned.'

"As I was being led out to the bier, I raised my head to heaven and pleaded silently for help. As we neared the burning fire, with hundreds of people standing round, I handed a package to a friend and said, 'Bring these to my father-in-law and say to him, "Take note, please, to whom do these belong, the signet and the cord and the staff?"' My father-in-law, shocked and ashamed, swallowed his pride, called off the death sentence, and proclaimed before the executioners and those standing around, 'She is more in the right than I, since I did not give her to my son Shelah.'"

"I gave birth to two sons, Perez and Zerah. Moses and Jesus are my descendants."

Tamar: A Woman of Courage

Tamar embodies the fulfillment of these words of Buber:

> Certainly, the relation of faith is no book of rules which can be looked up to discover what is to be done now, in this very hour. I experience what God desires of me for this hour . . . not earlier than *in* this hour. But even then, it is not given me to experience it except by answering before God for this hour as my hour by carrying out the responsibility for it towards him as much as I can.[13]

With Judah's refusal to give Shelah to Tamar as husband, Tamar was left with one of two choices: remain silent, which she did for a long time, or find a way to continue the Judah line of ancestors. So she did what she did as her only option, not knowing if her scheme would be successful.

In the book of Ruth it is written, "And may your [Boaz's] house be like the house of Perez whom Tamar bore to Judah— through the offspring which the Lord will give you by this young woman" (4:12).

In the Zohar, it is written, "Tamar, endowed with the gift of prophecy, knew that she was destined to be the ancestress of

---

13. Buber, *Between Man and Man*, 68.

David and of the Messiah, and therefore determined to fulfill her destiny."[14]

Tamar the Prophetess

Tamar became a prophet in listening to God speaking to her in the events of her life. She may not have known that God was speaking to her. She was simply true to herself, to the divine-human urges that welled up inside her. These divine-human urges are not easily discernible. One is faced with situations where one simply does not know what to do but can only take what seems to be the next right step, which leads to the next step, and the next step and the next. Through walking the road, one finds one's true road.

Decisions are the milestones in one's journey. We recognize the first big decision in Tamar's life when she decided to have a child by her father-in-law. That decision put her on the road to being burned alive. A second decision appears to have come directly from divine inspiration. She did not accept in payment the young goat from the flock without the pledge of Judah's signet ring, cord, and staff. It was this divine inspiration that saved her life and the twins in her womb when she was being led to be burned alive.

Tamar's life is a revelation to me of the interplay between the divine and the human. God urging, Tamar responding, without always knowing that she was responding to divine urges, for they were intertwined with her own human urges.

Tamar's life gives me courage to go to Rahab, the harlot mentioned in Matthew's genealogy. I ask if God spoke to her and how she may have responded.

RAHAB AND HER VISITORS

What has now approached me, the unforeseen, the unforeseeable, is word from him, a word found in no dictionary, a word that has now become word—and it demands my answer to him. I give the word of

14. *Encyclopaedia Judaica*, 15:783.

my answer by accomplishing among the actions possible that which seems to my devoted insight to be the right one.

–Martin Buber[15]

Now it is Rahab's turn to share her story with the other three women. Turning to them and looking at Tamar, she said, "Judah your father-in-law was indeed heroic to admit his fault. The Jewish people get their name from him. And you, dear sister, you were considered by the rabbis to be a vessel of the Holy Spirit.[16] You heard the Voice and with God you went forth. But now, for my story."

Rahab stood up. The women gasped. Rahab had not lost her beauty; she was known as the most beautiful woman in the world, the mere mention of her name exciting inordinate desire.[17] Exuding confidence yet compassion, she smiled and said, "You've all heard of me, Rahab, the harlot.

"My abode was situated in the wall of the city of Jericho, and it had a window on the outside. One night, when I was tired, two men knocked at my door wanting to stay for the night. I had no desire for them, but something pushed me to welcome them. The king of Jericho heard of my visitors and ordered me to deliver them to him. I felt that would be wrong to do; I don't know why, though I recognized them as feared Israeli spies. I took them in and hid them on the roof among the stalks of flax. I sent word to the king that I had received the men but they had left. And I added, 'If you pursue them, you should catch them.' The king's men pursued them. When night came, I let the spies down through the window. They were afraid. I said to them, 'Fear not. You are going to conquer the land. As my reward for protecting you, you must protect the whole of my family and me. And be easy with the other inhabitants, my kinsmen. Go toward the hill country; there the

15. Buber, *Between Man and Man*, 68.
16. Bereshit Rabbah 38:26.
17. Meg. 15a; Ta'an. 5b.

pursuers will not come upon you. Hide yourselves for three days, until they have returned; then afterward you may go your way' (Josh 2).

"The spies were saved and Joshua took possession of Jericho (Josh 6). My extended family was saved. I converted to Judaism and married Joshua. My descendants include a number of prophets and Jesus of Nazareth."

I ask, Did God speak to Rahab, the harlot?

> What has now approached me, the unforeseen, the unforeseeable, is word from him, a word found in no dictionary, a word that has now become word—and it demands my answer to him.[18]

Rahab heard a knock at the door. She opened the door, and recognized two Israeli spies. Should she welcome them or not? Without knowing quite why, she opened her door and welcomed them. Shortly thereafter, the king of Jericho heard that she had welcomed Israeli spies and ordered her to give them up. Now what should she do? She pondered all the pros and cons and decided to hide the spies. Before telling them how to save their lives, she made them promise that in the event of war, they would save her and her family. "I give the word of my answer by accomplishing among the actions possible that which seems to my devoted insight to be the right one."[19]

After Joshua conquered Jericho, he invited Rahab and her family to join Israel (Josh 6:25). In the Aggadah, Rahab is a righteous proselyte and marries Joshua and is the ancestress of eight prophets, among them Jeremiah and the prophetess Huldah. According to Matthew she married Salmon, the father of Boaz, who married Ruth and is the ancestress of Jesus (Matt 1:5).

In the New Testament it is said of her,

> By faith Rahab the prostitute did not perish with those who were disobedient, because she had given a friendly welcome to the spies. (Heb 11:31)

18. Buber, *Between Man and Man*, 68.

19. Buber, *Between Man and Man*, 68.

> And in the same way was not also Rahab the prostitute
> justified by works when she received the messengers and
> sent them out by another way? (Jas 2:25)

Rahab does not occupy a lot of space in the Bible, nor is she known for many exploits. The word that clings to her is that she was a prostitute. Yet God spoke to her in the present.

Multiple ways exist for God to talk to us, as many as the different events in our lives. God spoke to Eve in her encounter with a serpent. And God spoke to Abraham through his dissatisfaction. No one is excluded. God continues to talk to each of us in the present regardless of the way we have lived our lives up to that moment.

RUTH, LECH LECHA, "GO." (BOOK OF RUTH)

God's address to us penetrates the events in all our lives and all the
events in the world around us.

–Martin Buber[20]

Ruth is the third speaker to come forward. Her garments are the golden color of wheat, as is the beautiful kerchief tied loosely around her head. Her hair is wavy and dark brown. It matches her light brown eyes.

All are attentive. She begins, "There was a severe famine in the land. Starving, Naomi, my beloved mother-in-law, and her husband Elimelech decided to go with their two sons, Mahlon and Chillion, to my country, Moab, where food could be found.

"Not long after arriving, Elimelech died. I married Mahlon, and Chillion married Orpah. At the end of about ten years both of these sons died without offspring.

20. Buber, *I and Thou*, 182

"Naomi, feeling desolate, and hearing that the famine in Bethlehem was over, decided to return to Bethlehem. Orpah and I set out with her. At one point Naomi suddenly stopped. With tears in her eyes, she said, 'Turn back, my daughters, go your way, for I am too old to have a husband and give you sons to marry. It has been far more bitter for me than for you, because the hand of the Lord has turned against me.'

"Orpah kissed Naomi goodbye and left. I couldn't. I said, 'Do not press me to leave you or to turn back from following you! Where you go, I will go. Where you lodge, I will lodge. Your people shall be my people, and your God my God' (Ruth 1:16).

"Crowds met us as we entered Bethlehem. 'Is this Naomi?' they asked. Lifting up her head Naomi said,

> Call me no longer Naomi, call me Mara, for the Almighty has dealt bitterly with me. I went away full, but the LORD has brought me back empty; why call me Naomi when the LORD has dealt harshly with me, and the Almighty has brought calamity upon me? (Ruth 1:20–21)

"To stave off hunger I went out to the field to glean leftover ears of grain that had fallen from the reapers. Without knowing it, I came to a field that belonged to Boaz, a wealthy landowner of Bethlehem and a relative of Elimelech, Naomi's late husband. When he saw me, he asked others who I was. Then he came to me and said, 'Don't go to another field or leave this one. I've heard how you left your father and mother and your land and came to a people you did not know.' At mealtime he told me to come and eat with him and the reapers. After eating I went back to reap and I heard him tell the reapers, 'Let her glean even among the sheaves, and also leave some bundles aside for her.'

"In the evening, when I told Naomi what happened, her whole face lighted up and she said, 'The man is a close relative of ours.' Her words excited me. I continued reaping in his field until the end of the barley and wheat seasons.

"Naomi knew there would be a celebration to mark the end of the harvest. She said to me, 'Wash and anoint yourself, and put on your cloak. And go there but don't reveal who you are. After he has eaten and drunk and his heart is merry and he goes and lies down, go and uncover his feet and lie down.' My heart was pounding, but I did as she told me. At midnight Boaz woke up startled and asked who I was. When I told him, he said, 'May you be blessed. . . . You have made this last kindness greater than the first in that you have not gone after young men, whether poor or rich.'

"Then Boaz told me that a relative, according to the Levirate law (Ruth 4:1–12), had a right to me before him. He presented his case in such a way that the relative refused. We got married and I had a child.

"Women of the neighborhood came to Naomi and said, 'Blessed be the LORD who has not left you without kin. He shall restore life to you and be nourishment to you in your old age life, for your daughter-in-law who loves you, who is more to you than seven sons, has given birth to him' (4:15).

"And they named my child Obed. He became the father of Jesse, the father of David" (Ruth 4:17; Matt 1:5).

To Conclude

In my reading of the story of Ruth, I became more aware that God speaks to us through the events of our lives, events of both sorrow and joy. God gives no commands in this book. The characters take what seems to them to be the next right step in the situations they are in. This step led to steps that led to other steps that brought fulfilment.

First there is a famine. Naomi and Elimelech have to find food for themselves and their two sons, Mahlon and Chillion. They decide to go to Moab. While there, Elimelech dies. The two sons marry Moabite women, Mahlon, Ruth, and Chillion, Orpah. After about ten years in Moab the two sons die.

Naomi feels desolate. When she hears that the famine is over in Bethlehem, she decides to return home alone. Ruth loves her mother-in-law and insists on going with her.

Ruth needs to go to work to provide food for both of them. Boaz, a relative of Naomi, sees Ruth and is attracted to her. He ends up marrying her and they have a son whom they name Obed.

> And Salmon the father of Boaz by Rahab, and Boaz the father of Obed by Ruth, and Obed the father of Jesse . . . and Jacob the father of Joseph the husband of Mary, of whom Jesus was born, who is called Christ.
>
> So all the generations from Abraham to David were fourteen generations, and from David to the deportation to Babylon fourteen generations, and from the deportation to Babylon to the Christ fourteen generations. (Matt 1:5, 17)

Aware that God is talking to us is not a requirement to be faithful to God. Fidelity to one's authentic self is fidelity to God. God speaks to us in what we do, in the difficulties we have, in our sorrows and in our desires. God spoke to Ruth not in dissatisfaction as God spoke to Abraham, nor in discomfort as God spoke to Tamar, but through attraction, her deep love for Naomi, her mother-in-law. As I reflect on the lives of these personalities, I feel that the words of Tagore describe what was going on in their lives:

> Let only that little be left of my will whereby I may feel thee on every side, and come to thee in everything, and offer to thee my love every moment.[21]

In my next section I reflect on an episode in the life of Bathsheba who became the wife of King David after he killed her husband.

It is difficult to see how God could have anything to do with David after he murdered a just man or with Bathsheba, who married the man who killed her husband. Yet God did not abandon them, and they too are ancestors of the Jewish people and of Jesus of Nazareth.

---

21. Tagore, *Gitanjali*, 66.

BATHSHEBA: MOTHER OF KING SOLOMON
2 SAM 11–12; 1 KGS

Bathsheba stood. Tamar, Rahab, and Ruth gasped. Long black wavy hair tied with a bow flowed down her back. Pearl earrings dangled from her ears. She was wearing a white, loose-fitting chiffon gown with a low neck that revealed her shoulders and neck. She opened the Bible to the Gospel of Matthew and began to read chapter 1 in a serious but gentle voice. As she read, she accentuated the names of each of the women:

> An account of the genealogy of Jesus the Messiah, the son of David, the son of Abraham. Abraham was the father of Isaac, and Isaac the father of Jacob, and Jacob the father of Judah and his brothers, and Judah the father of Perez and Zerah by Tamar, and Perez the father of Hezron, and Hezron the father of Aram, and Aram the father of Aminadab, and Aminadab the father of Nahshon, and Nahshon the father of Salmon, and Salmon the father of Boaz by Rahab, and Boaz the father of Obed by Ruth, and Obed the father of Jesse, and Jesse the father of King David. And David was the father of Solomon by the wife of Uriah. (Matt 1:1–6)

Bathsheba put down the book and said, "There we all are: Tamar with her sons, Perez and Zerah by Judah; Salmon the father of Boaz by Rahab; and Boaz the father of Obed by Ruth; and David the father of Solomon by the wife of Uriah."

She took a step forward and repeated, "'David was the father of Solomon by the wife of Uriah.' That's me, Bathsheba. I was the wife of Uriah, whom David summoned after he saw me bathing on my rooftop. I became pregnant. My husband, Uriah, was a brave and faithful soldier in David's army. David sent for him. He gave him gifts and told him to rest and enjoy a few days of rest and comfort at home with me. But Uriah didn't come to me. When King David questioned him, he said, 'How can I do that while the other soldiers are camping in the open field.' David then invited him to dinner and got him drunk. But again he laid outside with the other servants. Then David sent him back to the army with a letter to

Joab, the commander, to put Uriah in the forefront of the hardest fighting so that Uriah would be killed. I mourned him for days.

"When the time of mourning was over, David took me as his wife. I gave birth to a weakling son who died. David was upset at the death of his son. He became more upset when Nathan, the Prophet, approached him, and said,

> Thus says the Lord: "Why have you despised the word of the LORD, to do what is evil in his sight? You have struck down Uriah the Hittite with the sword, and have taken his wife to be your wife, and have killed him with the sword of the Ammonites. Now therefore the sword shall never depart from your house, for you have despised me, and have taken the wife of Uriah the Hittite to be your wife." (2 Sam 12:9–10)

"David cried out, 'I have sinned against the Lord. Have mercy on me, O God, according to your steadfast love; according to your abundant mercy, blot out my transgressions'" (2 Sam 12:13).

David, the Repentant Sinner

David is celebrated as a warrior, prophet, musician, and lover. Yet he is also known as a cowardly sinner. From his affair with Bathsheba we have much to learn.

When he got Bathsheba pregnant, he did everything he could to have Bathsheba's husband, Uriah, appear as the father of the child. When that didn't work, he had her husband killed. Killing another man for personal reasons did not concern him. Thinking that Joab would be upset for the killing, he sent word to him, saying, "Do not let this matter displease you, for the sword devours now one and now another" (2 Sam 11:25).

Yet God did not abandon David for his crime. God sent Nathan the prophet to confront David with his sin. At the prophet's words, David awoke to the horror of his crime. According to tradition David cried out to God, "Have mercy on me, O God, according to your steadfast love and blot out my transgressions.

Wash me thoroughly from my iniquity, and cleanse me from my sin" (Ps 51:1–2).

God did not blot out his sins—they were engraved in his very being, and he himself had to deal with the punishments he brought upon himself. The prophet Nathan prophesied, "Now therefore the sword shall never depart from your house, because you have despised me and have taken the wife of Uriah the Hittite to be your wife" (2 Sam 12:10).

At a later time, David decided to build a house "to the name of the Lord my God." He said, "The house that is to be built for the Lord must be exceedingly magnificent, of fame and glory throughout all lands. I will therefore make preparation for it" (1 Chr 22:5). So David provided materials in great quantity.

Then David heard God speaking to him: "You have shed much blood and have waged great wars. You shall not build a house to my name, because you have shed so much blood before me on the earth" (1 Chr 22:8).

While David had to live with the crime he committed, God comforted him:

> See, a son shall be born . . . his name shall be Solomon . . .
> He shall build a house for my name. He shall be a son to
> me, and I will be a father to him, and I will establish his
> royal throne in Israel forever. (1 Chr 22:8–11)

David has gone down in history as a person after God's own heart (1 Sam 13:14; Acts 13:22). And Christians proclaim that Jesus was born into the house of David.

MOSES' ENCOUNTER WITH GOD (EXOD 3–4)

In the previous section I wrote of four questionable women honored in rabbinic literature as women upon whom the Holy Spirit rested. None of these women claimed that God spoke to them or directed them in their decisions, yet the rabbis credited them with being vessels of the Holy Spirit.

In this section I reflect on Moses' encounter with God. On one occasion, as was his custom, Moses led his father-in-law's sheep to the edge of the desert where he was faced with a bush that seemed to be on fire and yet was not consumed. Astonished, he drew near. A Voice called to him, "Moses, Moses." Moses replied, "Here I am." The Voice commanded, "Come no closer; remove the sandals from your feet. The ground on which you are standing is holy ground. I am the God of your father, the God of Abraham, the God of Isaac, and the God of Jacob." Terrified, Moses hid his face.

The Voice continued, "I have heard the cry of my people. I have come down to deliver them from the Egyptians. So come, now, I will send you to Pharaoh to bring my people, the Israelites, out of Egypt."

Awestruck, Moses thought, "That I can't do. No, I won't go back there. The Egyptians want me killed." Yet the Voice kept insisting, "I will be with you."

Facing the bush, he asked, "Who are you?' The Voice replied, *Ehyeh asher ehyeh*—this is my name forever, and this my title for all generations" (Exod 3:13–15). "*Ehyeh asher ehyeh!*" "What kind of a name is that?" Moses questioned.

Eyeh is a form of the Hebrew verb "to be." The dynamic name for God is YHWH. The first *ehyeh* in *Ehyeh asher ehyeh* stands for "*I am who I am;*" the second *ehyeh* refers to the future: "*I will be who I will be.*" The two *ehyeh's* in the same phrase say, *I am who I am, I will be who I will be.*[22] God, defined as YHWH (is—was—will be).

YHWH is in the now, was in the past when the past was now, and will be in the future. God addressed as God is the One who Is—Was—Will be.[23] Even when Moses had not encountered God, God was with Moses in all of his past. At the burning bush, Moses awoke to God's presence in the now.

Michael Fishbane, a modern-day Jewish scholar, called the event of Moses' encounter with God a "happening," a personal happening, a radical opening within Moses himself to a Divine Presence, triggered by the sight and awesomeness of the burning

22. Buber, *On the Bible*, 59.

23. Green, *Seek My Face*, 17.

bush. The ordinariness of his life, the guarding of the sheep in the silence of the wilderness, expedited this opening to an increased awareness of God as the heart and breath of all existence.

> The narrator presents this scene in a matter-of-fact way, for just this was the nature of Moses's life: it was simply matters of fact and easily portrayed in natural events. The circumstance is all silence. And suddenly it happens: from out of this stupor something uncanny appears to the shepherd's eye. At once everything is seeing and looking and appearing, and hardly matters of fact. The common has become spectacle, and there is a caesural opening (a pause, interruption) in the viewer himself, who decides to turn from his everyday tasks and behold the wondrous visage—at first out of sheer curiosity. It all occurs unexpectedly. A manifestation takes shape out of the vastness, revealing something of the mystery that can transfigure the natural world and set it off as holy.[24]

Moses was now settled in Midian with his father-in-law, a priest in Midian, who had seven daughters, one of whom, Zipporah, he married. Daily he took the flock of his father-in-law to pasture. He knew contentment. He knew peace. He enjoyed this hidden life after his stormy life in Egypt. He had no further desires—it was heaven for him. And then,

> Out of the depths the Divine breaks into human consciousness, but it cannot be fixed or formulated; it can only be attested to as a compelling presence, coming to be as it will be, again and again, and changing a person's life. The connection of this name with the fiery configuration that addressed Moses was momentary, but the truth he experienced went beyond this particular occurrence. From the divine side, God "shall be as God shall be" we are told, and one can say nothing further about it. Whereas from the human side, a person must simply be attentive to the vastness all around, for it is just here that God's affectivity

24. Fishbane, *Sacred Attunement*, 52.

inheres, and it may be experienced with such acuity as to seem supernatural to one's normal sensibility.[25]

When Moses brought the Israelites out of Egypt to Midian, to the place of the burning bush, at the foot of Mount Sinai, they too were caught up into a new world.

> The world is not just there as "a world," fixed and final but is rather a happening, ever coming into actuality through human attentiveness, and that the self, for its part is not just "a self," fixed in nature and proclivity, but a self-consciousness, ever attuned to itself and its worldly involvements. In this way the eruptive, caesural event is kept in mind by a new attentiveness to the contingency of experience, and an attunement to the deeper nature of worldly existence.[26]

They heard a Voice that said, "I am the LORD your God, who brought you out of the land of Egypt, out of the house of slavery" (Exod 20:2). Spontaneously, with gratitude and joy, they cried out, "All the words that the LORD has spoken we will do" (Exod 24:7).

The account of Moses at the burning bush is a poetic way of describing a "happening" in Moses' life where a radical opening took place within him. As he was guarding his father-in-law's sheep, behold, a veil was drawn aside. Suddenly, the ordinariness of everyday became extraordinary. He was in the Presence of God—he knew it, not with his head but with his whole being. He heard God addressing him and he heard his own replies. He asked the Presence, "Who are you; what is your name?" The reply, *Ehyeh asher ehyeh* (I am who I am, I will be who I will be) shook him. God was here, now, in this place. God was with Pharaoh's daughter warming her heart toward him floating on the Nile River. God was with Pharaoh when he warmed toward the babe and welcomed him into his household. God reminded Moses of the suffering Israelites held captive by Pharaoh. Then, he stood in shock again.

25. Fishbane, *Sacred Attunement*, 53–54.
26. Fishbane, *Sacred Attunement*, 19–20.

God said, "Come, I will send you to Pharaoh that you may bring my people, the children of Israel, out of Egypt" (Exod 3:10).

"No, not that, never!" he said within himself. As he wilted before the fact, he heard God say, "I will be with you . . . Now therefore go, and I will be with your mouth and teach you what you shall speak" (Exod 3:12; 4:12).

To be true to himself, Moses had to go. He set out for Egypt, with no idea how he could ever lead the Israelites out of Egypt.

CONCLUSION

O that today you would listen to his voice! (Ps 95:7)

I find the examples of these men and women in the Bible inspiring. What stands out for me is how they heard God speaking to them in their everyday lives. One would think that listening to God speaking to one in one's everyday life would make life easy. On the contrary, these biblical characters were faced with matters of life and death and came out victors, redeeming the situation.

"O that today you would listen to his voice!" (Ps 95:7). Will we? The church is faced with extinction unless it rids itself of a virus, known as anti-Judaism, which has riddled the church for centuries and turned Jesus' followers into collaborators with Hitler in the extermination of millions of Jews in Europe. Few Christians would see themselves in this role and would be horrified to hear that they were. I know my own horror when I remember the countless numbers of times I applied to all Jews statements about Jews found in the Gospels; for example, in John's Gospel:

> The Jews said to him, "Now we know that you have a demon!" (8:52)

> The Jews picked up stones again to stone him. (10:31)

> You [Jews] are from your father the devil, and you choose to do your father's desires. (8:44)

All Jews, down through the ages, have been accused of killing Jesus. In 1942, the Nietra Rebbe went to Archbishop Kametko of Nietra to plead for Catholic intervention against the deportation of the Slovakian Jews. The archbishop replied, "It is not just a matter of deportation. You will not die there of hunger and disease. They will slaughter all of you there, old and young alike, women and children, at once—it is the punishment that you deserve for the death of our Lord and Redeemer, Jesus Christ—you have only one solution. Come over to our religion and I will work to annul this decree."[27]

Such statements call for a reformulation of one's faith. The rabbis defined Judaism differently after the destruction of the temple in Jerusalem. It took a major flowering of Judaism and extraordinary spiritual leadership to articulate and restructure the tradition, and it was a painful, soul-searching, and highly conflictual process.[28]

Something similar needs to take place on the Christian side.

The Holocaust poses a devastating question to Christians: Can Jesus' name be redeemed in the church? Not unless we hear the Voice coming from the Shoah with the power with which it came from Sinai.

It follows that one of our first tasks is to study the history of the church with the Jewish people. That is the topic to which I now turn.

O that today you would listen to his voice! (Ps 95:7)

27. Greenberg, "Cloud of Smoke," 13.
28. Greenberg, "Cloud of Smoke," 24.

Chapter 3

My Encounter with Ecclesia and Synagoga

My mind often returns to the film *Crimes and Misdemeanors* by Woody Allen when I recall the Shoah, the Nazi destruction of the Jews in World War II, which was enabled in part by the church's demonization of the Jews. I ask, Can the church ever go back to normal after the Shoah?

In the film *Crimes and Misdemeanors*, Judah (Martin Landau), is faced with a major decision: Either confess his sin and live with the consequences or murder his mistress, who has become a liability to him. Judah's ophthalmologist, a rabbi, advises him to confess the sin and live with the consequences. He can't. He feels he will lose his prestige in the eyes of his wife and the community. After having his mistress killed, he is panic-stricken, on the verge of a mental collapse. Then one morning he wakes up, the sun is shining, and all seems right with the world. He takes his family on a vacation to Europe. Months pass and there is no punishment. His life is back to normal with all its privileges and acclaim. In the last scene, Cliff (Woody Allen, the director of the film) asks whether it can ever go back to normal. Judah replies, "Everyone carries a burden of sins. Maybe occasionally there's a bad moment, but then it passes. In time all fades." And Cliff replies, "I think it would be very difficult to live with that. Few guys could live with something like that on their conscience. Better to confess the crime and deal with the consequences."

Will the church confess the sins of its demonization of Jews down through the ages, which aided Hitler in his destruction of over six million Jews!

I entered the Sisters of Our Lady Sion (NDS) a Roman Catholic religious order, in 1944. We were founded by two Jewish brothers, Theodore and Alphonse Ratisbonne, converts to Catholicism. Theodore joined the church after a long search in 1826 and Alphonse, suddenly, as the result of a religious experience, on January 20, 1842. Both of them became ordained priests. They dedicated themselves to the conversion of Jews through prayer. Theodore, born in Strasbourg in 1802, wrote after his conversion, "My heart felt the need of inundating the children of Israel with the overflow of peace, light and happiness that I found." Though zealous for converts, Theodore Ratisbonne forbade, in the strictest terms, the Sisters to proselytize.

I came to know the Sisters of Sion as a student at the academy of Sion in Prince Albert, Canada, but I learned practically nothing of their unique mission. I never paid attention to the text on the lintel above the altar: "Father forgive them for they know not what they do" (Luke 23:34). The "they" were the Jews who crucified Jesus. Every Good Friday, we prayed the prayer of the church for their conversion:

> Let us also pray for the *perfidious* [emphasis mine] Jews, that our Lord and God may remove the veil from their hearts so that they too may acknowledge Jesus Christ our Lord. Almighty and everlasting God, you do not reject from your mercy even the *perfidy* of Jews; hear our prayer which we offer for the blindness of that people so that, having recognized the light of your truth, which is Christ, they may be rescued from their darkness.[1]

---

1. Lewis and Short's *Latin Dictionary* defines *perfidious*. It comes from the Latin *perifidus, per-fides*—that breaks his promise, unsafe, dangerous.

MY TIME OF SABBATICAL IN JERUSALEM

In the fall of 1978, the faculty of Theology, University of St. Michael's College (USMC), Toronto, gave me a two-year postdoctoral leave of absence. While one year was the norm, I asked for a second year. The question Jesus asked his disciples, "Who do you say that I am?" obsessed me. I was told that if I wanted an answer to that question I should go to Israel, live among the Jews, and walk where Jesus walked.

I enrolled in courses at the Ratisbonne Center, a center of Jewish studies for Christians. What I missed was circulating among the Jewish population. Then I heard that the municipality of Jerusalem was looking for teachers to teach English to bus drivers, soldiers, and other Jews who wanted to learn English. I offered my services at night school. This was a world-changing event for me. I met Holocaust survivors who shivered when they saw a crucifix. The crusades, inquisition, and expulsions of Jews were common knowledge for the ordinary Jewish citizen. I was driven by their experiences of the church to study the history of the church with the Jewish people. A door opened into a horror story.

Raul Hilberg,[2] in his book *The Destruction of the European Jews*, compared Vatican measures against the Jews with measures taken by Hitler and Nazi Germany:

Canon Law	Nazi Measure
*Prohibition of intermarriage and of sexual intercourse between Christians and Jews—Synod of Elvira, 306	*Law for the Protection of German Blood and Honor, September 15, 1935
*Jews and Christians not permitted to eat together—Synod of Elvira, 306	*Jews barred from dining cars—December 30, 1939

2. Hilberg, *Destruction of the European Jews*, 9. See also Parkes, *Conflict of the Church and Synagogue*; Flannery, *Anguish of the Jews*; Cohen, *Christ Killers*.

* Jews not permitted to show themselves in the streets during passion week—3rd Synod of Orleans, 538	*Decree authorizing local authorities to bar Jews from the streets on certain days—December 3, 1938
*Compulsory ghettos, Synod of Breslau, 1267 *Jews not permitted to obtain academic degrees, Council of Basel, 1434, Session XIX	*Law against overcrowding of German schools and universities, April 25, 1933

White Crucifixion, **by Mark Chagall, 1938**

Chagall's White Crucifixion links the Jewish Jesus, who is wearing a tallit (a Jewish garment) wrapped around his loins, to the persecution of Jews in the 1930s in Germany at the hands of the Nazis. In June and August of 1938, synagogues were destroyed in Munich and Nuremberg. Later that year on November 9, Kristallnacht (Crystal Night, Night of Broken Glass) more than 7000 Jewish stores and buildings had their windows broken, more than 1000 synagogues were desecrated, more than 30,000 Jews were arrested and sent to concentration camps and about 90 were killed. Kristallnacht marked the beginning of the Shoah.

Where can roots of such hatred towards the Jews be found?

In the writings of the fathers of the church, love of Jesus and hatred of the Jews were difficult to distinguish. St. John Chrysostom (347–407 CE), father and doctor of the church, gave eight homilies, *Adversus Judaeos*, to Christians in his congregation who were taking part in Jewish festivals and other Jewish observances. He wrote, "The synagogues of the Jews are the homes of idolatry and devils, even though they have no images in them";[3] "The very idea of going from a church to a synagogue is blasphemous";[4] "To attend the Jewish Passover is to insult Christ. To be with Jews on the very day they murdered Jesus is to ensure that on the day of Judgment He will say 'Depart from Me: for you have had intercourse with my murderers'. The Jews do not worship God but devils."[5] "God hates them, and indeed has always hated them."[6]

Such sermons prepared the ground for Hitler. On April 26, 1933, Hitler declared to Roman Catholic Bishop Wilhelm Berning of Osnabrück,

> I have been attacked because of my handling of the Jewish question. The Catholic Church considered the Jews pestilent for fifteen hundred years, put them in ghettos ... because it recognized the Jews for what they were. In

3. Chrysostom, *Eight Homilies*, 1.3; 2.3.

4. Chrysostom, *Eight Homilies*, 2.3.

5. Chrysostom, *Eight Homilies*, 1.3; 2.3.

6. Chrysostom, *Eight Homilies*, 2.3.

the epoch of liberalism, the danger was no longer recognized. I am moving back toward the time in which a
fifteen-hundred-year-long tradition was implemented. I
do not set race over religion, but I recognize the repre-
sentatives of this race as pestilent for the state and for the
Church, and perhaps I am thereby doing Christianity a
great service by pushing them out of schools and public
functions.

Hitler's claim that for fifteen hundred years the church considered Jews as a pestilence is borne out by the following overview
of the Catholic Church's relationship with and attitudes toward the
Jewish people.[7]

THE STRUGGLE BETWEEN OFFICIAL JUDAISM
AND THE JEWISH-CHRISTIAN CHURCH (55–313)

In the concrete lifetime of Jesus there is no separation between
Jesus and his followers and the Jewish community, for Jesus and
his followers were faithful Jews. Jesus was Jewish. He never repu-
diated his Jewishness. He went to the temple and the synagogue,
as did the other Jews. He was circumcised as a Jew. He spoke and
acted like a Jew. His mode of preaching and teaching were Jewish. Many of his parables and sayings can be found in Jewish tradition. His parents, Joseph and Mary, were Jewish. The apostles were
Jews. The women who announced the resurrection of Jesus were
Jews. The early members of the Jerusalem Church were Jewish.

The parting of the ways between Christianity and Judaism
took time. Tensions between Jewish and gentile followers of Jesus increased with the number of gentiles outweighing the Jewish
followers.

7. See Lichtenberg, *First to the Last of the Just.*

THE ERA OF CONSTANTINE (313–1096)

In 313 CE, the Roman emperor Constantine, after his unexpected victory at the Milvian Bridge in 312, issued the Edict of Milan, which granted Christianity legal status. From this time, emperors translated the theologians' concepts and claims about the Jews into practice. Ancient privileges granted to the Jews were withdrawn and the Jew was systematically banished from society. Paul Demann wrote that the process thus set in motion, with many detours and vicissitudes, reached its culminating point in a fully established Christianity, with its ghettos, its yellow badge (or its yellow cap), its humiliating restrictions, its vexatious measures, its multiple demands. This process left a deep mark on the social and psychological condition of the Jews in the countries heir to the Middle Ages.[8]

Vanquished by the empire and by the church, the Jews were portrayed in Christian statuary and iconography in the form of a defeated woman, her head bowed, her staff broken, her eyes blindfolded, and the Torah slipping from her hands. The church triumphant becomes "establishment" anti-Judaism.

THE BLOODY ERA OF THE CRUSADES (1096–1520)

The virus of hate and scorn that took root and developed in the church broke into a new frenzy during the time of the Crusades. The first Crusade of 1096 launched by Pope Urban II, the purpose of which was to recapture the Holy Places in Jerusalem from the Muslims, turned against the Jews. The crusaders of Rouen said that they wanted to fight the enemies of God in the East— but they had before their eyes the Jews, a race more the enemy of God than any other. Rouen, Poitiers, Treves, Worms, Mainz, Cologne, the crusaders, joined by an infuriated populace, pillaged, raped, sacked, massacred the Jews on their way to the liberation of the Holy Land. The route of the crusaders crossing the valley of the Rhine was strewn with corpses; forced baptisms,

8. Demann, *La Catéchèse Chrétienne.*

burnings, massacres were legion. The attempt of the civil or religious authorities to restrain this unleashing of passions had poor results.

The Fourth Lateran Council in 1215 under Pope Innocent III marked the peak of pontifical powers. Canons 67 to 70 of the Lateran Council contained anti-Jewish legislation. The Jews were forced to distinguish themselves from Christians by wearing the yellow badge or hat. They had to guard against any business contact with Christians. Christians were forbidden to give public office to Jews, thereby fixing the Jews in petty commerce, in money-lending, in barter or dealing in bric-a-brac. The image of the Jews as usurer and pawnbroker dates from this era when the occupations practiced until then—artisanry, agriculture, medicine—were closed to them.

The thirteenth century marked the birth of the Inquisition. It consisted of special tribunals charged with the defense of the Christian faith. Pyres were lit and prisons opened for all those suspected of heresy. The Spanish Inquisition became notorious for its pitiless persecution of the Marranos, Jews who had become Christian under duress and who maintained secret ties with Judaism. Statutes promulgated in Spain made "purity of blood" a new criterion for entry to certain guilds and to military and religious orders.

The fourteenth century was a period of great suffering for the Jews. They were blamed for wars, epidemics, and social upheavals of this time. They were blamed for the Black Plague that struck Europe in 1347. This constant blaming of the Jews sealed the fate of the Jew of Europe, around whose image in the eyes of the Christians, from then on, was a halo of sulphur and ashes. To exorcise this evil, the Jews were pillaged, massacred, chased from one country to another. Their expulsion in 1492, in the reign of the Catholic Queen Isabella, not only put an end to the story of the Jews of Spain but exemplified what more and more Christian countries did to the Jews within their precincts. The result for the Jews was that they retired into themselves, avoiding all relations with Christians.

In the thirteenth and fourteenth centuries, the "wall of separation" between Jews and Christians was barely penetrable.

THE COUNTER-REFORMATION PERIOD (1520–1789)

The spirit that characterized this period was one of resentment and retaliation by Christians and, more specifically, by the Catholic Church involved in this period in the struggle of the Counter-Reformation. The tribunals of the Inquisition continued to function in Spain until the nineteenth century. The Christian world of this period turned on the Jewish minority and held it responsible for the ills of society. Catholics laid the blame for the Protestant Reformation on the Jews; Protestants resented the Jews for not joining the march of the reform in Germany. This "anti-Semitism of retaliation" or of "resentment" explains the hardening of Christianity regarding the Jewish question.

EMANCIPATION AND ASSIMILATION: A NEW FORM OF ANTI-SEMITISM (1789–1945)

Gradual emancipation and assimilation of the Jews into society began fifty years before the French revolution. The Jews were given political rights in the countries where they existed. In these countries the Jews adopted the language and the culture of their environment; they were loyal to the state and identified themselves with the national feelings of their fellow countrymen. But by the second half of the nineteenth century a new form of anti-Semitism took shape. The basis was no longer religious but racial, the Nazi Holocaust being the most murderous of its manifestations.

In the words of Raul Hilberg,[9] "The missionaries of Christianity had said in effect: You have no right to live among us as Jews. The secular rulers who followed proclaimed: You have no right to

---

9. Hilberg, *Destruction of the European Jews*, 11.

live among us. The German Nazis decreed: You have no right to live."

Cardinal Walter Kasper, in his lecture on the relationship of the old and the new covenant as one of the central issues in Jewish-Christian dialogue, wrote, "Traditional theological anti-Judaism has cut the church off from its bearing and sustaining root, and has led to its impoverishment and weakening. This was one cause for the fact that most Christians did not oppose the crime of the Shoah with the resistance that one could have expected from them."[10]

WINDS OF CHANGE

The publication of *Nostra Aetate: Declaration on the Relation of the Church to Non-Christian Religions*,[11] was one of the most significant documents coming out of Vatican II.

Nostra Aetate had a difficult birth. It was hammered out in the full glare of the media with a sharp political dimension. What saved it were powerful forces before and during the session. Earlier forces date back to the 1930s in circles that included Jacques Maritain, Karl Barth, and James Park. James Park, a British Anglican clergyman, drew attention to how a whole culture of anti-Jewish prejudice had infected historical and Scripture studies.

The 1947 Seelisberg Conference that took place at Seelisberg in Switzerland on anti-Semitism, with sixty-three participants from twelve nations that included Jews, Protestants, and Roman Catholics, corrected wrongs and opened new doors. Its ten deliberations issued four calls to remember what Jews and Christians share in common (e.g., there is one God of Old and New Testament; Jesus was born a Jew; the first disciples, the apostles, and martyrs were Jews; the commandment to love God and one's neighbor is binding on both Christians and Jews) and six calls to avoid (e.g., distorting or misrepresenting biblical or post-biblical Judaism with the object of extolling Christianity; presenting the

10. Kasper, "Relationship of the Old and the New Covenant."

11. Paul VI, *Nostra Aetate*

passion in such a way as to bring the odium of the killing of Jesus upon all Jews or upon Jews alone; and teaching that the Jewish people are reprobate, accursed, reserved for a destiny of suffering).

A year after Seelisberg, the first General Assembly of the World Council of Churches declared that churches helped to foster an image of the Jews as the sole enemies of Christ which contributed to anti-Semitism in the secular world.

On October 28, 1958, Angelo Giuseppe Roncalli was elected pope and took the name John XXIII. As the papal nuncio in Bulgaria during the war, he helped to rescue many Jews from deportation to the death camps. He not only took direct action to rescue people, he denounced, before the Vatican and the Allied nations, the genocide carried out by the Nazis. After becoming pope, on Good Friday in 1959, he eliminated the words "perfidious Jews" from the Good Friday prayer. The universal church followed suit.

In 1959 he announced his call for the twenty-first ecumenical council of the Roman Catholic Church (1962–65). No one expected a rapprochement with the Jews to become one of the major achievements of the council. The visit of the Jewish historian Jules Isaac, author of *Jesus and Israel*, injected a new force into the thinking of Pope John. After his meeting with Jules Isaac, Pope John assigned Cardinal Bea to add "problems concerning the Jews" to his in-tray. Slowly and painfully *Nostra Aetate* came to birth (1965). Sect. 4 of the document emphasizes the bond between Christianity and Judaism; commits itself to foster mutual understanding and respect through biblical and theological studies and of fraternal dialogues; underscores God's special love for the Jewish people; and condemns hatred, persecutions, and displays of anti-Semitism at any time and by anyone.

Nostra Aetate opened the door to development. Pope Paul VI, elected after the death of Pope John XXIII, on October 22, 1974, established the Commission for Religious Relations with the Jews. Within a year of its foundation the Commission published its first official document with the title *Guideline and Suggestions for Implementing the Conciliar Declaration Nostra Aetate.*[12] The crucial

12. Vatican Commission, *Guidelines.*

and new concern of this document was its emphasis on gaining knowledge of Judaism as it defines itself. Eleven years later on June 24, 1985, the Commission issued a second document entitled *Notes on the Correct Way to Present Jews and Judaism in Preaching and Catechesis in the Roman Catholic Church*.[13] Among its many corrections was a note that declared that Israel was the "land of the forefathers," an "historic fact and a sign to be interpreted within God's design."[14] Previously, Pope Pius X on January 25, 1904, had said to Theodore Herzl, who sought the Vatican's support for the State of Israel, "The Jews have not recognized our Lord; therefore, we cannot recognize the Jewish people."[15] Then on December 30, 1993, the church broke with tradition and recognized the State of Israel.

At a press conference on March 16, 1998, Cardinal Cassidy, President of the Holy See's Commission for Religious Relations with the Jews, publicized the document *We Remember: A Reflection on the Shoah*.[16] In it, the church admitted its two-thousand-year relationship between Jews and Christians as regrettably negative.

The Pontifical Biblical Commission on May 24, 2001, published *The Jewish People and Their Sacred Scriptures in the Christian Bible*. It emphasizes the centrality of the Jewish Scriptures in the Christian Bible and illustrates the manner in which Jews are represented in the New Testament.

SION'S MISSION UNDERGOES TRANSFORMATION

As all these changes were taking place within the church, major changes were taking place among the Sisters of Sion in their understanding of themselves. On March 21, 1964, Sr. Laurice, head of the Sisters of Sion, asked the Sisters in charge of the centers of study and of the Archconfraternity of Prayer for Israel to suppress

13. Vatican Commission, *Notes*.

14. Vatican Commission, *Notes*, sect. 6.1.

15. Pope Pius X, in his meeting with Theodor Herzl, Jan. 25, 1904.

16. John Paul II, *We Remember*.

all their printed material on prayers for the conversion of the Jews. For those who had lived their lives praying for the Jews while hoping for their ultimate conversion, the request was wrenching.

That same year, Sr. Laurice heard that the unfinished document *Nostra Aetate* was about to be discarded. On August 4, 1964, she appointed Sr. Marie-Dominique Gros, general councillor, to write to the Sisters who worked in the Congregation's centers for Jewish-Christian relations and give them the mandate to contact bishops whom they knew. They were to do what they could to convince the bishops to support the document. They emphasized the need to make a clear statement that it was the Romans, plus some collaborating Jewish officials, who bore responsibility for Jesus' execution, not the people.

Sr. Marie-Dominque and Sister Magda, another member of the general council, became close collaborators with Fr. Bruno Hussar and others in writing draft material for what would become *Nostra Aetate* sect. 4, the section on the Jewish people. The entire document was approved on October 28, 1965.

How did a community of women who prayed daily for the conversion of the Jews evolve into a group that included a highly trained cadre who contributed to the writing of *Nostra Aetate*? The transformation was complex, beginning long before the Second Vatican Council and proceeding without a straight trajectory. In all the major centers of the Congregation of the Sisters of Sion— in Paris, London, Montreal, Sao Paulo, and Jerusalem—centers had been set up for the study of Judaism and dialogue with Jews. During the war, with no thought of conversion, Sisters of Sion, especially in Paris and Rome, helped hundreds of Jews escape the Nazis by giving them shelter and forged passports. After the war, a number of Sisters of Sion were listed among the righteous gentiles at Yad Vashem, the Holocaust Memorial Center, in Jerusalem.

In 1852, the Congregation of the Brothers of Sion was established, in partnership with the Sisters of Sion, with the same mission. The Brothers were catalysts in this new revolution. Paul Demann, born in Budapest in 1912 to an assimilated Jewish family, was baptized in 1934. In 1937, he joined the Brothers of Sion. In 1948 he started the *Cahiers Sioniens*, a periodical of the highest quality wherein topics related to Jewish-Christian relations and Judaism were discussed with theological and exegetical competence. He wrote not of the unfaithfulness of the Jews but of that of Christians who had persecuted Jews and thereby contributed to the Shoah. He was one of the Catholic participants in the Seelisberg Conference (1947). It was there he met Jules Isaac with whom he had a close relationship. The spread of *Cahiers Sioniens* and the Ten Points of Seelisberg were strong contributing factors in the radical revision of the church's attitude toward Jews and Judaism at the Second Vatican Council.

AN ABIDING SAD NOTE

One can only applaud the bold efforts of these statements to recognize and remedy the links between traditional Christian teachings and attitudes toward the Jews and the horrible anti-Semitism evident throughout European history and colonial expansion—links that became horrifically undeniable in Nazi Germany when "faithful and practicing" Christians had no qualms about their resolve and efforts to exterminate Jews.

And yet, and yet—the roots of anti-Judaism run deep in the Christian theology of supersessionism that still holds that the true role of "Old" Testament was to prepare for and be superseded by the New Testament. Anti-Judaism persists below the surface of firm condemnations of Auschwitz and inspiring recognition of the accomplishments of Jewish history.

The virus of supersessionist/replacement theology that has infected the church from its very beginning has *not* been sufficiently recognized nor remedied in these ecclesial documents. Indeed, such a subordination of the "Old" Testament to the "New" Testament is still alive, though not recognized, in general Christian attitudes and teachings today.

The fourth paragraph of *Nostra Aetate*, for instance, states that "As Holy Scripture testifies, Jerusalem did not recognize the time of her visitation." To affirm that Jews did not recognize the call of God in Jesus is to imply that they were *not* faithful to their desire to follow God's will. They have gone astray. That means that they are in need of being rerouted and converted.

The 1974 *Guidelines*, among its recommendations for correct interpretation of the New Testament, concludes that Jesus is "the fulfillment and perfection of the earlier Revelation."[17] This is a clear reaffirmation of supersessionism. For the Jews to refuse to be "fulfilled and perfected" by Jesus and Christianity means, again, that they are unfaithful and therefore stand as opponents to the gospel of Jesus.

The 1985 *Notes* stress that the mission of the church is to be "the all-embracing means of salvation" in which alone "the fullness of the means of salvation can be obtained." Again, to make such claims that Christianity, and only Christianity, has been given by God the "fullness" of truth and of the ways by which we are to know and serve God is to subordinate all the other expressions of saving truth. To realize the full reality of God's gift, one must become a follower of Jesus and the church. Those, like the Jews, who refuse may need to be respected, but they are clearly subordinated to the "only full" way to know God.

This virus of supersessionism, as I said, runs deep not only in the history of the European Christian churches but also in the founding Scriptures and traditions of Christianity. That is the topic of my next chapter.

---

17. Vatican Commission, *Guidelines*, sect. 2.

Chapter 4

Replacement Theology in Paul and the Gospels

IN MY SEARCH FOR the roots of anti-Judaism and anti-Semitism, I turn toward the New Testament, and I focus on Paul and the Gospels. In doing so, I am not digging for the pearls within the New Testament but for the viruses. As with any research into illnesses, the findings can be quite disturbing. Yet to ignore the problematic texts within the sacred books of any religion is to lessen the power of that religion to inspire men and women to love God and have hearts open to the whole of creation.

In this introduction I ask questions of when the epistles of Paul and the Gospels were written, by whom, and where. I am not able to list all my resources, for this has been a study of many years and much note taking.[1] I'm hoping that what I write will evoke questions, offer answers, and foster further study.

---

1. I am indebted to the following authors for this chapter: Dunn, *Jesus, Paul, and the Gospels*; Meier, *Marginal Jew*; Brown, *Introduction to the New Testament*; Fleischner, *Auschwitz*; Cook, *Modern Jews Engage the New Testament*.

Ecclesia and Synagoga at the double-portal of the south entrance to the Strasbourg cathedral. Both figures are of noble character. However, the church is depicted as triumphant with crown and imperial robe on her shoulders, with staff and chalice in her hands, symbolizing her divine authority. She looks ahead assured of her mission in the world. The synagogue is symbolized as defeated, her staff broken more than once, the Torah slipping from her hands, a veil covering her eyes, and her head bowed. Unknown artist, c. 1230.

The epistles of Paul (only half of the fourteen epistles attributed to Paul are genuinely his; the others were written by his disciples) were in circulation before the Gospels. They are dated mainly from the fifties. Paul wrote them for particular churches. Though addressed to circumstances specific to these communities, they have had a wide influence on later writings and teachings of the church.

The four Gospels were compiled at different times, one to two generations after the death of Jesus and of all those who knew him personally. The approximate dates for the final redaction of each of the Gospels are Mark: 72; Matthew: 85; Luke: 94; John: 100. The place of composition is disputed, but a general consensus is Mark in Rome, Matthew in Antioch, Luke in Greece, and John in Ephesus. The names of the authors (who were really editors) of the Gospels are pseudonyms—by the time the Gospels reached their final form all of Jesus' apostles were dead. The names Matthew, Mark, Luke, and John were prefaced to these Gospels at a later date to secure authority for them.

The Gospel of Mark is considered to be the first Gospel. It was a major source upon which Matthew and Luke drew. Despite the differences in time and composition Matthew and Luke repeat much of the same material found in Mark. For this reason, all three are called synoptic Gospels, meaning parallel reports—that is, they can be set out in parallel and looked at together, synoptically, "seen together."[2]

Most scholars[3] who have examined New Testament writings agree on the following: First, there was a historical person called Jesus who was born and lived in the land of Israel at the beginning of the Common Era. Second, this Jesus was a Jew, remained a Jew, and lived most of his life in Galilee. Third, he was a figure of influence and left a deep impression upon those who followed him. Fourth, he lived in an oral society. Though the Torah, the Prophets, and some of the Writings had long been in written form and were widely known by the Jewish population in Israel and abroad, still knowledge of them was spread orally. Recent studies of the first century show that during the Roman period, literacy was probably less than 10 percent. This small minority among the Jewish population would have been composed primarily of priests, Pharisees, and scribes (some scholars therefore hold that Jesus was probably illiterate). The widespread knowledge of the Torah would have been gained by people hearing the Torah read to them rather than by reading it themselves.

2. For authorship, context, and dates for the books of the New Testament see Brown, *Introduction to the New Testament.*

3. From personal notes of lectures and texts by Prof. James Dunn at Ben Gurion University, Beer Sheva, May 4–5, 2009.

Traditions about Jesus would likewise have been carried orally rather than through written texts. The editors of the Gospels knew these stories and used them as they composed their Gospel, but it wasn't a neutral writing. Each Gospel reflects the point of view of its editor and the needs of the church for which it was written. Hence, the Gospels give us not only a portrait of Jesus but also some understanding of the communities who gathered in his name. For example, the conflict expressed in the Gospels between Jesus and the Jews is more a reflection of the conflict that occurred between the young church and the synagogue at the time the Gospels were written. In the Gospels one has to distinguish between what Jesus could have said and done from that which comes from the theological stance of the author and the purpose for which the Gospel was written and the audience to whom it was addressed.

The earliest writings about Jesus in the New Testament are the letters of Paul. So to Paul I now turn.

PAUL AND REPLACEMENT THEOLOGY

For he who worked through Peter making him an apostle to the circumcised also worked through me in sending me to the Gentiles. (Gal 2:8)

Prior to Paul, what we now call Christianity was no more than a messianic sect within first-century Judaism, "the sect of the Nazarenes" (Acts 24:5). Without Paul this messianic movement might have remained a sect within Judaism and never become anything more than that. It was Paul who transformed this new Jewish sect that believed Jesus to be the Messiah into something more. The letters of Paul[4] are the only surviving sources from the first Christian generation. It is these letters that gave Christianity its new look.[5]

---

4. Recognized letters of Paul are 1 and 2 Corinthians, Romans, 1 & 2 Thessalonians, Galatians, Philippians, and Philemon.

5. Dunn, *Jesus, Paul, and the Gospels*, 119–20.

In what follows I deal with Paul and the replacement theology in his teachings on the Law, his metaphor of the olive tree, and his interpretation of "Israel."

The torah (also referred to as the law), and in particular the questions about circumcision and dietary laws, came under heated discussions between Peter and James, the acknowledged pillars of the Jerusalem church, on the one side, and Paul and Barnabas on the other. According to Paul, Jesus Christ replaced the Law:

> Yet we know that a person is justified not by the works of the law [the torah] but through faith in Jesus Christ. And we have come to believe in Christ Jesus, so that we might be justified by faith in Christ, and not by doing the works of the law, because no one will be justified by the works of the law. (Gal 2:16)

This is a shocking statement, for it comes from Paul, a self-proclaimed orthodox Jew. The turnabout in Paul's life was the revelation he had of Jesus Christ. Two different accounts exist of this experience: Paul's own account, which is found in his letters, and Luke's revised account in the book of Acts. Paul wrote (in the fifties),

> For I want you to know, brothers and sisters, that the gospel that was proclaimed by me is not of human origin; for I did not receive it from a human source, nor was I taught it, but I received it through a revelation of Jesus Christ. . . . But when God, who had set me apart before I was born and called me through his grace, was pleased to reveal his Son to me, so that I might proclaim him among the Gentiles, I did not confer with any human being, nor did I go up to Jerusalem to those who were already apostles before me, but I went away at once into Arabia, and afterwards I returned to Damascus. Then after three years I did go up to Jerusalem to visit Cephas [Peter] and stayed with him fifteen days; but I did not see any other apostle except James the Lord's brother. In what I am writing to you, before God, I do not lie! Then I went into the regions of Syria and Cilicia. (Gal 1:11–23)

Luke's account, written about forty years after the death of Paul, is a revision of Paul's account. Luke describes Paul's experience by putting words into his mouth:

> I am a Jew, born in Tarsus in Cilicia, but brought up in this city at the feet of Gamaliel, educated strictly according to our ancestral law, being zealous for God, just as all of you are today. I persecuted this Way up to the point of death . . . as the high priest and the whole council of elders can testify about me. From them I also received letters to the brothers in Damascus, and I went there in order to bind those who were there and to bring them back to Jerusalem for punishment. While I was on my way and approaching Damascus, about noon a great light from heaven suddenly shone about me. I fell to the ground and heard a voice saying to me, "Saul, Saul, why are you persecuting me?" I answered, "Who are you, Lord?" Then he said to me, "I am Jesus of Nazareth whom you are persecuting." . . . I asked, "What am I to do, Lord?" The Lord said to me, "Get up and go to Damascus; there you will be told everything that has been assigned to you to do." Since I could not see because of the brightness of that light, those who were with me took my hand and led me to Damascus. A certain Ananias, who was a devout man according to the Law . . . came to me; and standing beside me, he said, "Brother Saul, regain your sight! . . . the God of our ancestors has chosen you . . . you will be his witness to all the world of what you have seen and heard." (Acts 22:3–15; see also Acts 9:1–22)

Luke's edited account of Paul's experience with the risen Jesus is the better-known version among Christians. Paul's own words differ sharply from those of Luke. Paul describes a solitary personal experience of the risen Jesus that took place in Damascus, not on the road to Damascus. There is no mention of being commissioned by the high priest. What he learned was not of human origin, nor did he receive it from a human source, nor was he taught it, but he received it through a revelation of Jesus Christ. When he went up to Jerusalem, three years after his return to Damascus from Arabia, he was still unknown by sight to the leaders of the Jesus movement.

While there, he had a short visit with Peter for fifteen days and another short visit with James, the brother of Jesus. From this we can assume that Paul had little knowledge of the historical Jesus.

None of Paul's letters focus on the historical Jesus. He wrote nothing about Jesus' teaching, his miracles, his parables. He rarely used the name "Jesus" (only about 4 percent of his references use the name "Jesus"). His interpretations of Jesus were based on his experience of the resurrected Jesus, not on the historical Jesus. His references to Jesus are in cosmic terms: "Christ Jesus our Lord," "his Son, Jesus Christ our Lord."

A Transformative Experience

Paul's vision had a profound effect upon him. In his words, his former life appeared as rubbish:

> Yet whatever gains I had, these I have come to regard as loss because of Christ. More than that, I regard everything as loss because of the surpassing value of knowing Christ Jesus my Lord. For his sake I have suffered the loss of all things, and I regard them as rubbish, in order that I may gain Christ. (Phil 3:7–8)

He lived in agony, under the burden of his sins:

> I am of the flesh, sold into slavery under sin . . . sin that dwells within me . . . nothing good dwells within me . . . in my flesh. I can will what is right, but I cannot do it . . . I see in my members another law . . . making me captive to the law of sin . . . Wretched man that I am! Who will rescue me from this body of death? (Rom 7:14–24)

Such statements were unheard of among law-abiding Jews who knew of atonement through the temple cult of sacrifice. But Paul was not of Jerusalem; he was born in Tarsus and lived most of his life in the Jewish diaspora. He blames the law for his awareness of his sin:

> If it had not been for the law, I would not have known sin. I would not have known what it is to covet if the law

had not said, "You shall not covet." But sin, seizing an opportunity in the commandment, produced in me all kinds of covetousness. (Rom 7:8)

Paul and the Law

Though Paul claimed to be a faithful Jew, he did not find the law (the Jewish way of life) a *way to salvation*. In his letter to the Galatians he wrote,

> For through the law, I died to the law, so that I might live to God. I have been crucified with Christ; and it is no longer I who live, but it is Christ who lives in me. And the life I now live in the flesh I live by faith in the Son of God, who loved me and gave himself for me. (Gal 2:19–20)

Paul had harsh language to his followers who wanted to observe the Jewish commandants:

> For all who rely on the works of the law are under a curse; for it is written, "Cursed is everyone who does not observe and obey all the things written in the book of the law." Now it is evident that no one is justified before God by the law; for "The one who is righteous will live by faith." (Gal 3:10)

In following verses, Paul adds,

> For freedom Christ has set us free. Stand firm, therefore, and do not submit again to a yoke of slavery. Listen! I, Paul, am telling you that if you let yourselves be circumcised, Christ will be of no benefit to you. Once again, I testify to every man who lets himself be circumcised that he is obliged to obey the entire law. You who want to be justified by the law have cut yourselves off from Christ; you have fallen away from grace. (Gal 5:1–4)

Paul was radically changed by his vision of the risen Jesus:

> For I decided to know nothing among you except Jesus Christ and him crucified. (1 Cor 2:2)

> And be found in him, not having a righteousness of my
> own that comes from the law, but one that comes through
> faith in Christ. (Phil 3:9)

It is clear from Gal 1:1, 3–14 that Paul regarded his way of life within Judaism as something past. As a Christian, he would no longer describe himself as "in Judaism."[6] His followers followed suit. They came to believe that the law (the Jewish way of life) had no value for them.

The Metaphor of the Olive Tree

Since the Jewish people did not accept Jesus as their Messiah, Paul asked, "Has God rejected his people?" He replied, "By no means" (Rom 11:1). They will only be blind for a short while—for now God gave them "a sluggish spirit, eyes that would not see and ears that would not hear" (Rom 11:8), in order to bring salvation to the gentiles. Once the gentiles have been grafted into the natural olive tree in great numbers, the conversion of Israel to her Messiah will bring even greater blessings to the world: "And so all Israel will be saved" (Rom 11:26).

> You will say, "Branches [the Jews] were broken off so
> that I [gentiles] might be grafted in." That is true. They
> were broken off because of their unbelief . . . And even
> those of Israel, if they do not persist in unbelief, will be
> grafted in, for God has the power to graft them in again.
> (Rom 11:19–20, 23)

The figure of the olive tree emphasizes that gentile salvation is dependent on Israel's covenant relationship to God. Gentiles are wild branches that have to be grafted into the natural olive tree to be saved. The purpose of the gentile influx into the natural olive tree is not merely for the salvation of gentiles, but to evoke envy on the part of Israel as a way of leading Israel to recognize Jesus as the promised Messiah. That is to say, the gentiles are saved not merely

---

6. Dunn, *Jesus, Paul, and the Gospels,* 122.

for their own sake, but for the sake of Israel. But as we know, Paul's hope for his people was not realized.

Did God Reject God's People?

In Paul's words, the church is the legitimate continuation of Israel, but that does not mean that God rejected Israel. Paul comes to this conclusion in different ways. First, they will be grafted back into their tree when they come to believe in Jesus the Messiah—they were broken off because of their "unbelief." Second, because of "the remnant," who recognize Jesus. For him, Israel is not the whole of the people: "For not all Israelites truly belong to Israel" (Rom 9:6). Paul explains: God's promises never applied to all of Israel (Rom 9:6–13). God chose Isaac instead of Ishmael, the rightful heir (Gen 17:19–21) and God chose Jacob instead of Esau, the rightful heir (Gen 25, 26). That is, Israel according to the flesh and Israel according to the promise! Many who ethnically belong to Israel do not belong to the Israel of God's promise and many who do not belong to the Israel of the flesh (gentiles) belong to the Israel of the promise. That is to say that those Jews, the "remnant" who accept Jesus as the promised Messiah comprise authentic Israel. The "old" Israel, those Jews who refuse to believe in Jesus, have lost their privileged position as God's specially chosen people.

To Conclude

For Paul, the Jesus movement, under his leadership, was the continuation of Judaism. He was deeply sad that all the Jews did not accept Jesus as the Messiah:

> I have great sorrow and unceasing anguish in my heart.
> For I could wish that I myself were accursed and cut off
> from Christ for the sake of my own people, my kindred
> according to the flesh. (Rom 9:2–3)

Yet he comforted himself, for "from them [the Jews], according to the flesh, came the Messiah, who is over all, God blessed forever. Amen" (Rom 9:5). Yet at other times, Paul himself wrestled with, and was uncomfortable with, such "replacement" of the Jews—as is evident in Rom 11.

It was Paul's theology that led to the parting of the ways between the Judaism that Jesus lived and Christianity.

Dunn writes,

> Paul was the one who transformed this Jewish sect which believed Jesus to be the Messiah into something more. Paul's mission and the teaching transmitted through his letters did more than anything else to transform embryonic Christianity from a messianic sect, quite at home within Second Temple Judaism, into a religion hospitable to Greeks, increasingly Gentile in composition . . . And it is these letters which ensured that Paul's legacy would continue to influence and indeed give Christianity so much of its definitive character . . . it was Paul's mission which made it impossible for Gentile believers to be retained within the traditional forms of Judaism, and because his writings became the most influential reinterpretations of the original traditions and forms of the new movement.[7]

MARK AND REPLACEMENT THEOLOGY

Cardinal Walter Kasper, in a 2002 lecture, bemoaned the traditional theological anti-Judaism that cut the church off from its bearing and sustaining root (Judaism) and led to its impoverishment and weakening. He regretted that most Christians did not oppose the crime of the Shoah with the resistance that one should have expected from them. "How," he asked, "could such barbarism be possible in a continent shaped by a long Christian tradition?" It is now time, he urged, for full repentance on the part of Christians and for historical and thorough theological reflection.[8]

7. Dunn, *Jesus, Paul, and the Gospels*, 121–22.

8. Kasper, "Commission for Religious Relations."

These words are before me as I reflect on the Gospel according to Mark, the first Gospel written, which Matthew and Luke relied upon for their Gospels. I look for passages in Mark's Gospel that could have led the church to see itself replacing the Jews as God's chosen people.

It is difficult to consider one's sacred writings as having anything in them that is not God's revelation. Yet we Christians have plenty of examples of texts in our Scriptures that denigrate others. To recognize such problematic texts and to deal with them will make Christianity a better instrument for building the kingdom of God on earth. Irving Greenberg, reflecting on the history of contempt for Jews on the part of Christians, wrote, "There is an alternative for those whose faith can pass through willingness and who have the ability to hear further revelations and reorient themselves."[9]

In his Gospel, Mark assures his gentile Christians that they are the authentic inheritors of the Jesus legacy, for according to him, the Jewish disciples of Jesus abandoned him in his last days and one of them actually turned him in to the Roman authorities. His Gospel, with the epistles of Paul, laid the basis for conceiving of Christianity as "the fulfillment and perfection of the earlier Revelation [Judaism]."[10]

The Editor of Mark's Gospel

Though the writer of Mark's Gospel is unknown, we do know something about his Gospel. It is dated in the late sixties or early seventies of the Common Era, thirty to forty years after the death of Jesus, in the aftermath of the First Jewish Revolt against Roman rule in Judaea (66 CE) and around the time of the destruction of the temple by the Romans in 70 CE.

Mark himself was a gentile follower of Jesus who lived in Rome (though some say in Syria). He wrote in Greek to an audience composed of a majority of gentile followers of Jesus and a

9. Greenberg, "Cloud of Smoke," 24.

10. Vatican Commission, *Guidelines*, art. 3.

minority of Jewish followers. This mix was problematic for Mark, as it was for Paul. We can imagine the Jewish followers of Jesus saying, "Jesus was a Jew. He was circumcised. He observed the Sabbath. He went up to the temple for Passover. He taught in the synagogues. If you want to be a follower of Jesus you must keep the law." Such a call was bad news for the Greek followers of Jesus who did not follow the Jewish way of life.

Mark didn't know Jesus. What he knew was by hearsay. He adapted and recast what he heard in order to fit his audience's knowledge and needs. Like all the other gentile members of his community, he was not familiar with Aramaic, the language of Jesus. So he translated into Greek Aramaic words that were attributed to Jesus—for example, *Talitha cum* ("Little girl, get up," 5:41); *Ephphatha* ("Be opened," 7:34); and Jesus' cry from the cross, *Eloi, Eloi, lama sabachtani?* ("My God, my God, why have you forsaken me?" 15:34).

The Authentic Inheritors of the Jesus Legacy

In confrontation with the Jewish followers of Jesus, the gentile followers wanted to know who were the authentic guardians of the Jesus legacy. Was it the acknowledged pillars of the Jesus movement, Peter, James, and John and their followers, who now were a minority? Or was it Paul, who described himself as an apostle to the gentiles (Gal 2:7–9, Rom 11:13), the one who set the Jesus movement off in another direction?

At the time of Mark's writing, Jews and Romans were enemies. Gentile followers who associated with Jews were not looked kindly upon by their fellow citizens. As a consequence, gentile followers of Jesus pulled further away from Jews and Jewish practices. Mark's Gospel assures them that they are the authentic followers of Jesus.

One of the ways he did this was to show that those closest to Jesus, his family, his own apostles whom he chose, did not understand him. They did "not comprehend" (4:13; 6:52; 7:18; 8:18–21), did "not understand" (8:31–33), were "hard of heart" (8:17), were blind and deaf (8:18), and all deserted him in his moment of dire need (14:50), including Peter who denied knowing him (14:68).

He also described the Jews as preferring their traditions over God's commandments. When some of the Pharisees asked Jesus why his followers did not live according to the traditions of the elders, Mark's Jesus replied, "Isaiah prophesied rightly about you hypocrites, as it is written, . . . 'You abandon the commandment of God and hold to human tradition. You have a fine way of rejecting the commandment of God in order to keep your tradition! . . . thus, making void the word of God through your tradition that you have handed on. And you do many things like this'" (Mark 7:6–13).

Mark supported those who did not observe the Jewish kosher laws of clean and unclean foods. According to him, Jesus said, "'Do you not see that whatever goes into a person from outside cannot defile, since it enters, not the heart but the stomach, and goes out into the sewer?' (Thus he declared all foods clean.)" (Mark 7:8–19). This, of course, is questionable. If Jesus had really proclaimed all foods fit for consumption, the Pauline letters and Luke's book of Acts, would never have struggled with the question whether gentile followers of Jesus needed to keep the Jewish dietary laws.

With these arguments, Mark supported his gentile followers as the authentic followers of Jesus.

The Death and Passion of Jesus

According to Mark, not the Romans but the Jews are responsible for the crucifixion of Jesus. The chief priests, mentioned sixteen times in Mark 14–15, were the chief actors in Jesus' death. It was they who whipped up the Jewish crowds to clamor for his death. Mark doesn't tell us that the chief priests were under the power of Rome, making it historically impossible for the Jewish authorities to act on their own in tracking down Jesus and arresting him.

An important issue in Mark's Gospel is his seeming creation of additional characters. Judas is one of these. The name is suspect. He is not mentioned in any of Paul's writing. The sound of the word "Judas" suggests an intentional equation between Judas and

Jew. In Greek, *Ioudas* (Judas) and *Ioudaios* (Jew) have the same sound. It was Judas, the Jew, a disciple of Jesus, who betrayed him to the chief priests. No motive is given why Judas would betray Jesus (that is filled in by other Gospel writers).

Other Gospel writers, writing much later than Mark, used his Gospel as a main source of their versions of the life and message of Jesus. They took the Judas story and elaborated on what they found missing in Mark. Matthew suggests the reason for the betrayal was greed, thirty pieces of silver (26:15). Since that is not a sufficient reason for Luke (22:3) nor for John (6:70; 13:2, 27; 17:12), they have Satan enter Judas and propel him to do what he did. In Matthew, Judas in remorse hangs himself—a strange act after he has repented (27:3–5). The account in Acts (1:18) suggests that Judas used the money to buy a field, but then ended up committing suicide in it.

If Judas is a creation of Mark, why would Mark have created him? A probable reason is to attach the blame for Jesus' death onto the Jewish nation whose name Judas bore. Not only was it Judas, the Jew, who betrayed Jesus, but Judas as the Jews betrayed Jesus.

Barabbas is the other likely creation of Mark.

> Now at the festival he used to release a prisoner for them, anyone for whom they asked. Now a man called Barabbas was in prison with the rebels who had committed murder during the insurrection. So, the crowd came and began to ask Pilate to do for them according to his custom. Then he answered them, "Do you want me to release for you the King of the Jews?" For he realized that it was out of jealousy that the chief priests had handed him over. But the chief priests stirred up the crowd to have him release Barabbas for them instead. Pilate spoke to them again, "Then what do you wish me to do with the man you call the King of the Jews?" They shouted back, "Crucify him!" Pilate asked them, "Why, what evil has he done?" But they shouted all the more, "Crucify him!" So, Pilate, wishing to satisfy the crowd, released Barabbas for them; and after flogging Jesus, he handed him over to be crucified. (15:6–15)

Such a scene is problematic. No record exists in history of releasing a prisoner at the time of Passover. What would be the point of such a release when the meal was over?

To Conclude

When we consider Mark's treatment of the Jews in his Gospel, we are shocked. But shock can act as a purifying agent that will enable us to sort the grain from the chaff. Cardinal Kasper, as noted above, gave a push in this direction when he bemoaned the traditional theological anti-Judaism that cut the church off from its sustaining roots and pleaded for ecclesial repentance—which begins with recognition of the evil.

MATTHEW AND REPLACEMENT THEOLOGY

Therefore I tell you, the kingdom of God will be taken away from you and given to a people producing its fruits. (Matt 21:43)

Matthew's Gospel has been referred to as both the most pro-Jewish and the most anti-Jewish Gospel. References can be found in the Gospel for both assessments. If the Gospel is examined in light of how it has influenced church history, it is a most anti-Jewish Gospel and a Gospel of replacement. In what follows I examine both of these appraisals—why Matthew's Gospel can indeed be considered to be pro-Jewish and at the same time anti-Jewish. Then I will look at some parables that portray the kingdom of God taken away from the Jews and given "to a people that produces the fruits of the kingdom" (Matt 21:43).

The Gospel reveals different levels of composition, an early version that is pro-Jewish and a later one where the Jews are cast aside.

The final redaction of the Gospel was in Greece, around 85 CE. It was composed in Antioch. We don't know the author. The name Matthew was the name assigned to the Gospel at a later date; the redactor was evidently an anonymous gentile follower of Jesus.

As the final editor, he drew material from earlier editions. In the final edition, as we have it today, the Gospel includes 92 percent of the Greek edition of Mark and 51 percent of Mark's very words. Matthew doesn't hesitate to edit Mark's Gospel to emphasize his own teachings addressed primarily to gentile followers.

Pro-Jewish and Anti-Jewish Levels

Matthew ends chapter 4 with the notice that great crowds followed Jesus from Galilee, the Decapolis, Jerusalem, Judea, and from beyond the Jordan. When Jesus gathered the crowds together, he said,

> Do not think that I have come to abolish the law or the prophets; I have come not to abolish but to fulfill. For truly I tell you, until heaven and earth pass away, not one letter, not one stroke of a letter, will pass from the law until all is accomplished. Therefore, whoever breaks one of the least of these commandments, and teaches others to do the same, will be called least in the kingdom of heaven. (Matt 5:17–19)

In this earlier stage, Jesus sees his mission as limited solely to the Jews. When his disciples embark on a first mission he charges them, "Go nowhere among the Gentiles, and enter no town of the Samaritans, but go rather to the lost sheep of the house of Israel" (Matt 10:5–6). And when a Canaanite woman begs him to heal her daughter, he replies to her, "I was sent only to the lost sheep of the house of Israel" (Matt 15:24). The gentiles are "them." Jesus warns his disciples not to be like "them." "When you greet others, don't greet only your brothers and sisters, for do not even the Gentiles do the same?" (Matt 5:47). When praying, Jesus says, "Do not heap up empty phrases as the Gentiles do; for they think that they will be heard because of their many words" (Matt 6:7). And do not worry about your lives, what you will eat, and what you will wear, "for it is the Gentiles who strive for all these things; and indeed, your heavenly Father knows that you need all these things" (Matt 6:32).

Torah observance is important to Jesus. Surrounded by crowds of people and his disciples, Jesus said, "The scribes and the Pharisees sit on Moses' seat; therefore, do whatever they teach you and follow it; but do not do as they do, for they do not practice what they teach" (Matt 23:1–3).

When gentiles became the majority in the church, roles are reversed. In Jesus' time the gentiles are referred to as "them." In Matthew's time, the Jews are the "them." Mark 3:1 has Jesus enter "*the* synagogue." In Matt 12:9 it becomes "*their* synagogue." Mark 6:2 has Jesus begin "to teach in *the* synagogue." In Matthew 13:54, it is "*their* synagogue." Matthew laments that the allegation of a theft of Jesus' body from the tomb "has been spread among *the* Jews to this day" (28:15)—not among us or our fellow Jews.

While the beginnings of the "church" in Antioch may have been composed mostly of Jewish followers of Jesus, by Matthew's time it had become a gentile movement, enabled by the visit and teachings of Paul. It was in Antioch that the followers of Jesus were first called Christians (Acts 11:26).

The execution of James, the brother of Jesus, in Jerusalem, and the Jewish revolt against Rome in 66, weakened the centrality of Jewish leadership in Jerusalem and elsewhere. Fear, hate, and mistrust spread between Jews and gentiles. This was especially felt in Antioch where the lives of Jewish followers were put in jeopardy. Josephus[11] informs us that hatred of the Jews was everywhere at its height—in Antioch they were harassed, even murdered by gentiles who spread rumors of Jewish plots and asked the Roman general, Titus, to expel Jews, or at least to revoke their privileges. The result was a diminishing of the balance of power between the Jewish and the gentile followers of Jesus with gentile followers in the ascendancy.

The break between the Jewish and gentile followers of Jesus is visible in Matthew's editing of Mark's Gospel:

11. Josephus, *New Complete Works*, 593.

Mark 12:28ff.	Mathew 22:35ff.—revising Mark
One of the scribes . . . asked him, "Which commandment is the first of all?"	One of [the Pharisees], a lawyer, asked him a question *to test him.* "Teacher, which commandment in the law is the greatest?"
Jesus answered, "The first is, 'Hear, O Israel: the Lord our God, the Lord is one; and	He said to him,———
you shall love the Lord your God with all your heart, and with all your soul, and with all your mind, and with all your strength'" . . .	"You shall love the Lord your God with all your heart, and with all your soul, and with all your mind. This is the greatest and first commandment."
Then the scribe said to him, "You are right, Teacher; you have truly said that 'he is one, and besides him there is no other'" . . . Jesus . . . said to him, "You are not far from the kingdom of God."	———

In Matthew's editing of the Shema, the first line of which is, "Hear, O Israel," Matthew has a Pharisee *testing* Jesus (indicative of growing tension between Jesus and the Jewish leaders) and he deletes Mark's opening sentence, "Hear, O Israel, the Lord our God, the Lord is one" (which no Jew, including Jesus, would have deleted).

The Jews Lose Their Privileged Position

In the parable of the vineyard, Jesus tells the Pharisees the kingdom of God will be taken from the Jews and given to a more worthy nation:

> There was a landowner who planted a vineyard, . . . leased it to tenants and went to another country. When the harvest time had come, he sent his servants to the tenants to collect his produce. But the tenants seized his servants and beat one, killed another, and stoned another. Again he sent other servants, more than the first; and they treated them in the same way. Finally he sent his son to them, saying, "They will respect my son." But when the tenants saw the son, they said to themselves, "This is the heir; come, let us kill him and get his inheritance." So they seized him, threw him out of the vineyard, and killed him. Now when the owner of the vineyard comes, what will he do to those tenants? They said to him, "He will put those wretches to a miserable death, and lease the vineyard to other tenants who will give him the produce at the harvest time." Jesus said . . . "Therefore, I tell you, the kingdom of God will be taken away from you and given to a people that produces the fruits of the kingdom." . . . When the chief priests and the Pharisees heard his parables, they realized that he was speaking about them. (My adaptation of Matt 21:33–45)

According to an interpretation of this parable and other parables, God's covenant with the Jewish people does not endure. It is transferred to "a people that produces the fruits thereof."

The last line of this parable gives the clue to the identity of those mentioned: The tenants are the Jews, the servants are the prophets, and the son is Jesus. With that in mind, let us reread this parable:

> *God . . . planted a vineyard, . . . leased it to Jews . . . When the harvest time* had come, he sent the Hebrew prophets to collect his produce. But the Jews seized the Hebrew prophets and beat one, killed another, and stoned another. Again he sent other Hebrew prophets, more than

the first; and they treated them in the same way. Finally he sent his son Jesus to them, saying, "They will respect my son." But when the Jews saw the son Jesus, they said to themselves, "This is the heir; come, let us kill him and get his inheritance." So the Jews seized him, threw him out of the vineyard, and killed him. Now when . . . God . . . comes, what will he do to the Jews? They said . . ."God will put those wretches to a miserable death, and lease the kingdom of God to Gentiles who will produce the fruits of the kingdom" . . . When the chief priests and the Pharisees heard his parables, they knew very well that he was speaking about them.[12]

A second parable, that of the banquet (Matt 22:1–14), has a similar message. Jesus said, "The kingdom of heaven may be compared to a king who gave a wedding banquet for his son." The invited guests (the Jews) did not respond to the king's invitation. Angry, the king commanded, "Go therefore into the main streets, and invite everyone you find."

The Jews lost their privileges. Jesus warns his disciples to "beware of the yeast (teachings) of the Pharisees and Sadducees (Matt 16:6). For emphasis the command is repeated (Matt 16:11–12). These leaders are "hypocrites, children of hell, blind guides, blind fools, children of those who murdered the prophets, serpents, brood of vipers" (Matt 23). (Such condemnations would be utterly offensive and denigrating to any Jew, follower of Jesus or not).

The composition of the church has become gentile. Matthew's Jesus foretold it. One day a centurion stopped Jesus in Capernaum and asked him to heal his servant who was in terrible distress. Jesus replied, "I will come and cure him." The centurion replied, "I'm not worthy of that. Just say the word and my servant will be healed." Jesus, astounded at his faith, replied,

Truly I tell you, in no one in Israel have I found such faith. I tell you, many will come from east and west and will eat with Abraham and Isaac and Jacob in the kingdom of heaven, while the heirs of the kingdom [the Jews] will be thrown into the outer darkness. (Matt 8:10–12)

12. Cook, *Modern Jews Engage the New Testament*, 199.

Matthew's Jesus bewails the loss of his people: "Jerusalem, Jerusalem . . . How often have I desired to gather your children together as a hen gathers her brood under her wings, and you were not willing" (Matt 23:37).

To Conclude

Matthew's description of Pilate in chapter 27 lays the blame for the crucifixion of Jesus upon the Jews. In Matthew, Pilate, a ruthless leader, who executed any suspected Jewish rebel at the drop of a hat, is transformed into a caring Roman magistrate who felt sorry for a falsely accused Jew.

Pilate asks the Jews, "Whom should I release, Barabbas[13] or Jesus?" for he realized it was out of jealousy that they had handed him over. And the Jews said, "Barabbas." Pilate asked, "Why, what evil has he done?" And the Jews shouted all the more, "Let him be crucified." Then Pilate took water and washed his hands before the crowd (the Jews) and said, "I am innocent of this man's blood; see to it yourselves." And the Jews replied, "His blood be on us and on our children" (Matt 27:24–25). This response, put into the mouth of the Jews, has fueled anti-Judaism down through the ages.

Matthew's Gospel ends with his final declaration:

> Then Jesus cried again with a loud voice and breathed his last. At that moment the curtain of the temple was torn in two, from top to bottom. The earth shook, and the rocks were split. (Matt 27:50–51)

It's the final announcement of the end of the Old Covenant and the beginning of the New Covenant.

13. There was no such custom among the Romans or Jews of releasing someone during Passover. It was an invention of Mark's Gospel, and used by Matthew to exonerate the Romans and blame the Jews. See Chavel, "Releasing of a Prisoner."

LUKE AND REPLACEMENT THEOLOGY

Then both Paul and Barnabas spoke out boldly, saying, "It was necessary that the word of God should be spoken first to you [Jews]. Since you reject it and judge yourselves to be unworthy of eternal life, we are now turning to the Gentiles." (Acts 13:46)

Luke's Gospel is a Gospel I loved because he presents Jesus as a faithful Jew. But after years of studying this Gospel, I have come to the sad conclusion that Luke loves Judaism but hates the Jews.

The book of the Acts of the Apostles was also composed by Luke. The Gospel focuses on Jesus the Jew and his ministry, and the book of Acts on Paul and the history of the early church. Throughout these two books Luke insists that Christianity embodies and continues authentic Judaism, while Jews in rejecting Jesus as their Messiah orphaned themselves from their own heritage.

The final redaction of Luke's writings took place in Greece around 90–94 CE, about two decades after the destruction of the temple in 70 CE, some fifty years after Jesus' death, and about thirty years after Paul's death (around 64 CE).

In what follows I deal first with Luke's presentation of Jesus and lastly with Christianity as the embodiment and continuation of authentic Judaism.

Luke's Presentation of Jesus

Jesus a Faithful Jew: In Luke's Gospel, Jesus and his followers are Jews. This is clear in the number of scenes or reports unique to Luke and not at all found in the other Gospels. Luke tells us of the circumcision of the infant Jesus (2:21) and the story of his parents "doing what was customary under the law" (2:22, 27) by bringing him to the temple in Jerusalem for the redemption of the first-born ceremony. The holy family journeys annually to Jerusalem to celebrate Passover; on one of these journeys, when Jesus was twelve and lost, his family found him in the temple, the central place of Jewish liturgical worship, listening to the sages and asking them questions (2:41-49). As an adult Jesus continued to go to the temple and he taught there daily (19:47, 21:37) and regularly in their synagogues (4:15). He observed the Sabbath—he went to the synagogue on the Sabbath day, as "was his custom." After his death, the women rested "according to the commandment" on the Sabbath day before going to the tomb to anoint the body of Jesus (23:56). After Jesus' resurrection, his followers "were continually in the temple" (24:53).

Jesus Son of David: During the height of King David's power, it was thought that God would choose a descendant of David to reign over Israel forever. During Roman times, the Jews looked for a descendent of David to free them from Roman oppression.[14] In first-century Christianity there was a strong belief that Jesus was of Davidic descent. Numerous references in the Synoptic Gospels and the book of Acts refer to Jesus as the son of David: Mark 10:47; 12:35–37; Matt 9:27; 12:23; 15:22; 20:30; 21:9, 15; 22:42–45; Luke 3:31; 18:38–39; 20:41–44; Acts 2:25–31; 13:22–23.

Paul, in his letter to the Romans, announced himself as an apostle for the gospel of God, the gospel concerning his Son, "who was descended from David according to the flesh and was declared to be Son of God with power according to the spirit of holiness by resurrection from the dead, Jesus Christ our Lord" (1:3–4). In Acts, Peter addresses the crowd and says,

> Fellow Israelites, I may say to you confidently of our ancestor David that he both died and was buried, and his tomb is with us to this day. Since he was a prophet, he knew that God had sworn with an oath to him that he would put one of his descendants on his throne. Foreseeing this, David spoke of the resurrection of the Messiah, saying, "He was not abandoned to Hades." (Acts 2:29)

This is to say that Jesus, as the "seed of David" and in his resurrection from the dead, fulfilled the promise God made to David in 2 Sam 7:12–14: "I will raise up your offspring after you . . . and I will establish his kingdom . . . and I will establish the

---

14. *Encyclopaedia Judaica*, 11:1407.

throne of his kingdom forever. I will be a father to him, and he shall be a son to me."

Jesus the Promised Messiah: Luke begins his Gospel with the nativity story. An angel appeared to shepherds who were keeping watch over their flock at night and said, "Do not be afraid, for see—I am bringing you good news of great joy . . . to you is born this day in the city of David a Savior, who is the Messiah, the Lord" (2:11).

It was not difficult to pass from an understanding of Jesus as son of David to Jesus the Messiah, the anointed one. The two names, son of David and Messiah, are often joined together. In Luke's Gospel, Jesus challenged the scribes with the question, "How can they say that the Messiah is David's son?" (Luke 20:41). Before Luke, in Matthew's Gospel, Jesus asked the Pharisees, "What do you think of the Messiah? Whose son is he?" They said to him, "The son of David" (Matt 22:42). And later, Mark wrote that while Jesus was teaching in the temple, he asked, "How can the scribes say that the Messiah is the son of David?" (Mark 12:3–5).

Earlier followers of Jesus believed that he was the Messiah though he did not conform to the political expectations Jews had for the Messiah. At first, Jesus' disciples were demoralized by his crucifixion, but after coming to believe that he had been raised from the dead, their hopes were rekindled in the expectation that he would soon come back to complete his mission. Luke makes three claims about Jesus' Jewishness: that Jesus is a faithful Jew, that he is of the seed of David, and that he is the promised Messiah. Together these claims are Luke's way of declaring that Christianity embodies authentic Judaism.

Luke's Interpretation of Paul

The best place in Acts to judge Luke's genuine views toward the Jews is in passages he assigns to Paul. Why, I ask, does Luke center Paul's life and activities in Jerusalem when Paul himself doesn't? As I wrote above, Luke, who wrote some thirty years after the death of Paul, transformed Paul, a diaspora Greek-speaking Jew born in Tarsus (present day Turkey), into a Jerusalemite. He reports that Paul studied in Jerusalem at the feet of Gamaliel, a teacher of the law and respected by all the people (Acts 5:34–35), and that he was sent on mission to Damascus by the high priest and the whole council of elders in Jerusalem. In Paul's personal account we learn that Paul had a personal solitary experience of the risen Jesus in Damascus, not on the road to Damascus, that he was not sent by the high priest, and that only three years after his experience did he go up to Jerusalem where he was "still not known by sight" (Gal 1:22).

The likely reason Luke stressed the centrality of Jerusalem in Paul's mission is his need to have Paul recognized as sent from Jerusalem, the heart of Judaism, to strengthen his argument that Christianity was in continuity with Judaism.

Christianity Embodies and Continues Authentic Judaism

According to Luke, it was not the followers of Jesus who broke with Judaism, but the Jews who refused to accept Jesus as their Messiah. Luke put words into the mouth of Paul to emphasize this:

> Then both Paul and Barnabas spoke out boldly, saying,
> "It was necessary that the word of God should be spoken
> first to you. Since you reject it and judge yourselves to
> be unworthy of eternal life, we are now turning to the
> Gentiles." (Acts 13:46)

> When they opposed and reviled him, Paul in protest
> shook the dust from his clothes and said to them, "Your
> blood be on your own heads! I am innocent. From now
> on I will go to the Gentiles." (Acts 18:6)

A number of Luke's parables tell how the Jews lost their privileged position with God. The parable of the great dinner closes with these words: "For I tell you, none of those [Jews] who were invited will taste my dinner" (Luke 14:24).

In the parable of the vineyard (Luke 20:9–19), a repetition of Matthew's account, the tenants (the Jews) are destroyed for killing "the son" (Jesus). To the question, what will the owner of the vineyard do to them, they reply, "He will come and destroy those tenants and give the vineyard to others." The parable ends with the words "the scribes and chief priests realized that he had told this parable against them."

Once Again: A Conundrum

We are faced again with the painful reality that rejection of the Jews was built right into the biblical text. In fact, it appears that Luke emphasizes Jesus' Jewishness in order to use it as a tool to condemn the Jews. Jesus, the faithful Jew, was not recognized—indeed, was rejected—by his fellow Jews.

And so, for Luke, Jews lost their birthright as God's chosen people. They were replaced, superseded by the new chosen people. In Jesus' time, Jesus-followers were all Jews and continued with their traditional practices of temple worship and ritual cleanings. But that changed. The beginning of "the parting of the ways" is reflected in Paul's teaching that his followers should live by faith in Jesus Christ and not in the law.

So again, we face the question: how to overcome the present day divisions of Christians and Jews based on a theology of supersessionism when its roots run so deep in the New Testament itself?

JOHN AND REPLACEMENT THEOLOGY

Replacement (in John's Gospel) is a sign of who Jesus is, namely, the one sent by the Father who is now the only way to the Father. All previous religious institutions, customs and feasts lose meaning in his presence.

–RAYMOND BROWN[15]

---

15. Brown, *Gospel*, 104.

I used to love the Gospel according to John, as do many others, because of its deep spirituality. In this post-Shoah era, however, I now read this Gospel with very different eyes. I've come to the conviction that if we want to save this Gospel as a deeply inspiring text, we have to deal with supersessionism, which lurks within it—that is, with the claim that the church has replaced the Jewish people as God's chosen people.

In the first part of what follows, I deal with John's characterization of the Jews and in the second part, with "supersessionism" in his Gospel.

The word "Jews" is used in John's Gospel more than seventy times and mostly in a negative manner. The final redaction of the Gospel was written in Greek and completed in Ephesus (Asia Minor, modern day Turkey) around 100 CE, about seventy years after Jesus' death. The words Jesus are said to have spoken underwent extensive transformations during those seventy years.

This doesn't mean that we can't find authentic words of Jesus in this Gospel, but we must remember that neither Jesus nor his followers left any written documents. The impact Jesus had on followers kept his memory alive. But his words were often adapted and even enlarged upon by the different Gospel writers—this is clearly evident in Jesus' long discourses at the Last Supper in John's Gospel.

No one knows the name of the final editor of John's Gospel. The Gospel is a combination of the writings of different editors. The name John, in memory of John, Jesus' beloved disciple, was attached to the final edition to give it authority. The earlier layers are pro-Jewish; later layers are filled with vilification of Jews. A change of Gospel editors can be distinguished by a change of expressions, e.g., "our" Passover becomes "the Passover of the Jews" (6:4) or "a festival of the Jews" (5:1; 6:4; 7:2).

The Jews: Who Are They in John's Gospel?

Adele Reinhartz[16] wrote that the earlier layers of John's Gospel have an overall Jewish feel. Jesus and his followers live according to the Jewish calendar. They observe Sabbath and the festivals (e.g., 2:13; 5:9), and they congregate within the temple and the synagogue (6:9; 7:14). When Jesus discusses matters of Jewish law, he relates his discussion to the torah (5:39; 6:32). He follows Jewish customs such as ritual handwashing before meals (2:6), and giving thanks for bread before eating a meal (6:11). After his death, his disciples anoint his body and cover him with a shroud according to Jewish custom.

In later layers his opponents are the Jews, e.g., "Pilate replied, 'I am not a Jew, am I? Your own nation and the chief priests have handed you over to me. What have you done?'" (18:35).

Are All the Jews Implicated in John's Gospel?

Several New Testament scholars deal with the question of whether or not all the Jews were implicated in the death of Jesus. Some interpret the word "Jews" in John's Gospel to refer to the chief priests and Pharisees. Others claim that the word "Jews," *Ioudaioi* in Greek in its plural form, refers only to the Judeans who lived in Judea. Reinhartz[17] disagrees with both of these stances. For her, the word "Jews" is not limited to a small group within Judaism but to Jews in general.

She reminds us that John wrote his Gospel around the end of the first century CE, a time when *Ioudaioi* was a term used to denote "Jews" in general. The writer refers to them in the third person, for example, "The Passover of the Jews was near and Jesus went up to Jerusalem" (2:13). All are included in John's references to the Jewish festivals (2:13; 5:1; 6:4; 7:2; 11:55); even the water

16. Fredriksen and Reinhartz, *Jesus, Judaism, and Christian Anti-Judaism,* 102.

17. Fredriksen and Reinhartz, *Jesus, Judaism, and Christian Anti-Judaism,* 112.

jugs in use at Cana were for Jewish rites of purification (2:6) and references to burial customs are references to Jewish burial rites. In other words, John's use of the word "Jews" seventy times, mostly in a negative form, implicates all Jews.

Why Was Jesus Crucified?

According to John's Gospel he was crucified by the Jews for blasphemy and for breaking the law:

> The Jews were seeking all the more to kill Jesus, because he was not only breaking the Sabbath but was also calling God his own Father, thereby making himself equal to God. (5:18)

Pontius Pilate, the Roman governor, carried out the crucifixion at the Jews' request. Pilate questioned Jesus as to what he had done, for "your own nation and the chief priests have handed you over to me" (18:35). After he questioned Jesus, he "went out to the Jews," and said to them, "I find no case against him" (18:38). At these words, the chief priests shouted, "Crucify him! Crucify him!" Pilate said, "Take him yourselves and crucify him." The "Jews" responded, "We have a law, and according to that law he ought to die because he has claimed to be the Son of God" (19:7).

Supersessionism, Replacement Theology in the Gospel According to John

Again, my question: Has Christianity, in the Gospel of John, replaced Judaism? Raymond Brown says yes. Brown summarizes the theme of the first ten chapters of John's Gospel in this manner: Chapters 2 through 4 present the replacement of Jewish institutions and religious views, and chapters 5 through 10 are dominated by Jesus' actions and discourses on the occasion of Jewish feasts, often again by way of replacing the motif of the feasts. Jesus is the real temple; the Spirit he gives will replace the necessity of worshiping at Jerusalem; his doctrine and his flesh and blood will give life in a way that the manna associated with the Exodus from Egypt did not; at the Feast of Tabernacles, not the rain-making ceremony but Jesus himself supplies the living water; not the illumination in the temple court but Jesus himself is the real light; on the Feast of the Dedication, not the temple altar but Jesus himself is consecrated by God.[18]

Brown supports his conclusions with reflections on different scenes in John's Gospel:

1. Changing water into wine at the wedding at Cana. This is the first sign (2:1–11). Jesus and his disciples are invited to a wedding in Cana, a village that is in walking distance from Nazareth. The whole village seems to have been invited. At the entrance to the wedding place six stone water jugs stand, each holding twenty to thirty gallons of water, equaling about a hundred and fifty gallons, for the purification rites of the guests as they arrive. At one point during the celebration Mary, Jesus' mother, notices that the wine has run out. Believing in Jesus' power, she informs him of the embarrassing situation. Jesus hesitates, yet to please his mother he tells the waiters to fill the jars with water. When done, a waiter fills a glass. Behold not water but wine! The waiter hands the glass to the steward, who pauses, sniffs its exceptional aroma, and then tastes it. He calls the bridegroom and exclaims, "Everyone serves the good wine first, and then the inferior wine after the guests have become drunk. But you have kept the good wine until now."

The water changed into wine was not from regular sources of drinking water but from the six stone water jugs used for Jewish purification rites. It's this water that is changed into wine, a sign that the old age is gone; the new age has arrived.[19]

2. Healing the royal official's son in Capernaum (4:46–54). A Roman official whose son lies ill in Capernaum heard that Jesus had arrived back in Cana. He set out to beg Jesus to heal his son, though the journey was long—about a day's trip by donkey, today about forty-five minutes by car. Upon seeing him, Jesus said, "Go, your son will live." Believing in Jesus, he turned around and began

18. Brown, *Gospel*, 104.

19. Brown, *Gospel*, 104–11.

the journey home. Before he was halfway home, his servants met him and announced, "Yesterday at one in the afternoon the fever left him." That was the hour when Jesus said, "Go, your son will live." So he himself believed, along with his whole household.

It's an outsider and his whole family who come to believe in Jesus while those of his own nation do not: "But to all [the outsiders] who received him, who believed in his name, he gave power to become children of God" (1:12). These outsiders (gentiles) become the insiders, and the insiders (the Jews) become the outsiders.[20]

3. Healing of the paralytic at Bethesda (5:1–15). After Jesus healed the official's son, he went up to Jerusalem, a distance today of about one hundred forty-five kilometers, to attend the festival of Shavuot. Upon arrival he went over to the pools by the Sheep-Gate. Its five porticoes were crowded with sick people (remnants of ancient pools are visible in the courtyard of St. Anne's Church in the Muslim quarter of Jerusalem). Jesus approached a paralytic who had frequented these pools over thirty-eight years—no one helped him to get into the pool when the waters were miraculously stirred. Jesus looked with compassion upon him and said, "Stand up, take your mat and walk." The man whom the waters could not heal was cured by Christ.[21]

4. The miraculous feeding of the five thousand (6:5–31). An unbelievably large crowd gathered on the other side of the sea, across from Tiberius, to a place where food was unavailable. A boy with five loaves of bread and two fish gave them to Jesus to feed the hungry. Jesus took the bread and the fish, blessed them, and gave it to the crowd. When all were satisfied, twelve baskets of food remained.

Astounded, the crowd called out, "This is indeed the prophet who is come into the world." When Jesus realized that they were about "to come and take him by force to make him king, he withdrew again to the mountain by himself" (6:14–15).

---

20. Brown, *Gospel*, 190–98.

21. Brown, *Gospel*, 211.

Later, when the crowd met again with Jesus, they said, "Our ancestors ate the manna in the wilderness; as it is written, 'He gave them bread from heaven to eat'" (6:31).

Jesus replied,

> Your ancestors ate the manna in the wilderness, and they died. This is the bread that comes down from heaven, so that one may eat of it and not die. I am the living bread that came down from heaven. Whoever eats of this bread will live forever; and the bread that I will give for the life of the world is my flesh. (6:49–51)

Jesus is the living bread that replaces the manna in the desert.

5. Walking on the water (6:16–24). The disciples were on the Sea of Galilee, headed for Capernaum, when a terrible storm blew up across the lake. As a huge wave was about to swallow them up, they saw Jesus walking on the water. Jesus called out to them, "It is I (*Ego eimi*); do not be afraid." *Ego eimi*, "I Am" is the name God gave to the divine Self when Moses asked God for God's name. God replied, "I Am," in Greek, *ego eimi* (Exod 3:14). Brown questions whether the Evangelist equates Jesus with God by these words. He argues at some length that the much-discussed phrase, *ego eimi*, is not, as some have argued, a declaration that Jesus is identified with God. *Ego eimi* is

> more a description of what he is in relation to man. In his mission Jesus is the source of eternal life for men (*vine, life, resurrection*); he is the means through whom men find life (way, gate); he leads men to life (shepherd); he reveals to men the truth (truth) which nourishes their life (bread) . . . Jesus is these things because he and the Father are one (are united, 10:30) and he possesses the life-giving power of the Father (5:21).[22]

And it is precisely this role, this mission, of Jesus as God's son and spokesperson that, according to John, "the Jews" refused to recognize. In their decision not to recognize him as God's Son they cut themselves off from *the vine* that can give them eternal

---

22. Brown, *Gospel*, 534–35.

life; they refuse to follow *the way* that will lead them to truth; they turn their backs on the Good Shepherd; they cut themselves off from the Bread of Life.

And so, for John, the Jews were blind for not recognizing Jesus as their Messiah. Their refusal broke the special relationship they had with God. Jesus' followers were the new Israel. John summarizes their plight succinctly and tragically: "Those who believe in him are not condemned; but those who do not believe are condemned already, because they have not believed in the name of the only Son of God" (John 3:18).

6. Healing a man born blind at the Pool of Siloam (9:1–7). The pool of Siloam in Jerusalem is southeast of the Temple Mount. It was considered a pool of living water. During the seven-day Festival of Sukkot (Feast of Tabernacles) a unique ceremony of water-drawing was performed every morning. A priest would take a golden vessel to the pool (Siloam), fill it with water, and bring it back to the altar accompanied by flute players and carriers of torches of fire while the crowd joyfully sang the Hallel Psalms (113–118). According to the Talmud,[23] "Whoever has not seen the rejoicing at the Place of the Water-Drawing has never seen rejoicing in life."

On one occasion, during the festival Jesus saw a man blind from birth at the pool of Siloam. His disciples asked him, "Rabbi, who sinned, this man or his parents, that he was born blind?" Jesus said, "He was born blind so that God's works might be revealed in him." When he had said this, he bent down, took soil from the earth and with his spittle made mud, which he rubbed on the man's eyes, saying to him, "Go, wash in the pool of Siloam—which means Sent" (John 9:7).

That the evangelist pauses to interpret the name of the pool where the healing water was obtained and gives the explanation that the name means "one who has been sent" associates the water with Jesus. Jesus is the one who has been sent. He is the source of living water.[24]

23. Sukkah 5:10.

24. Brown, *Gospel*, 381.

7. The ideal shepherd versus the wicked shepherds.

> So again, Jesus said to them, "Very truly, I tell you, I am the gate for the sheep. All who came before me are thieves and bandits; but the sheep did not listen to them. I am the gate. Whoever enters by me will be saved, and will come in and go out and find pasture. The thief comes only to steal and kill and destroy. I came that they may have life, and have it abundantly. I am the good shepherd. The good shepherd lays down his life for the sheep." (10:7–10)

This parable of the good shepherd and the sheepgate follows immediately after Jesus' attack on the Pharisees in chapter 8. No new audience is suggested. The real point of the parable is that of entering through the gate, which is Jesus. All must pass through the gate that is Jesus in order to be saved; he has come to bring life to the sheep. The Pharisees and Sadducees, the most probable targets of Jesus' remarks, are thieves and bandits who avoid entering through the gate (10:8).

In summary: John's Gospel is a Gospel of replacement of the Jews by Christianity. John's use of the title "the Jews" more than seventy times, mostly in a negative manner, came to implicate all Jews and opened the floodgates to anti-Judaism and anti-Semitism. As the disease of hate spread, John was referred to as the "father of anti-Semitism" and his Gospel, a Gospel of "Christian love and Jew hatred."[25]

So once again we are confronting hatred, denigration, and demonization of the Jewish people built right into and, indeed, integral to one of the Four Gospels. We are not dealing with a "misreading" or abuse of the text. This is what the text says and proclaims: The Jews, in rejecting Jesus the Messiah and Son of God, now have the devil for their father (John 8:44). Unless they convert and recognize the one and only Son of God, they have no right to be called "children of God" (John 1:12). No other way exists for them to God (John 3:36; 14:6).

25. Cook, *Modern Jews*, 219.

This is the challenge that faces all Christians: what to do when the "revelation of God" in the New Testament calls for the demonization of an entire people.

CONCLUSION

Within our inspired and ancient scriptures lies the revealed Jesus truth, but it is enmeshed within its own archaic context. Thus, those scriptures contain much that we today *cannot accept as divine truth.*

–John Keenan[26]

Most religions look upon their sacred books as texts written under divine inspiration. But though they are divinely inspired, they are still written by human hands, which means they are subject to human weaknesses and cultural limitations. This is also true of the New Testament. Because it is a divine/human book we need to dig within this human soil to sift and distinguish the truth of divine revelation from the often distorting, cultural, and human limitations of its historical context. Such interaction of our biblical texts with contemporary questions and awareness can cast light upon misrepresentations and can open doors to new understandings.

Since the Shoah, the murder of six million Jews, churches of different denominations have examined and admitted that their "teachings of contempt for the Jews" contributed to this tragedy. The Catholic Church published several documents[27] on this topic that reveal an about-turn in its relationship with the Jews. These documents condemn hatred, persecutions, displays of anti-Semitism directed against Jews at any time and by anyone. Yet despite all that has been written, *the church has not dealt with supersessionism and the replacement theology* that is the original

26. Keenan, *Earthing the Cosmic Christ*, 73.

27. Paul VI, *Nostra Aetate,* Vatican Commission, *Guidelines*, sect. 4; Vatican Commission, *Notes*; Pontifical Biblical Commission, *Jewish People*.

and continuing source for Christianity's "contempt of the Jews." On the contrary, such supersessionist theology has been sustained in ongoing language about the church as the fulfillment of Judaism and the replacement of the old Israel.

I repeat again, in *Nostra Aetate* sect. 4, it is stated, "As Holy Scripture testifies, Jerusalem did not recognize the time of her visitation." *Guidelines*, among its recommendations for correct interpretation of the New Testament, concludes that Jesus is "the fulfillment and perfection of the earlier Revelation."[28] *Notes* stress that the mission of the church is to be "the all-embracing means of salvation" in which "*alone* the fullness of the means of salvation can be obtained."[29] *The Jewish People and Their Sacred Scriptures* encapsulates the church's teaching on supersessionism/replacement theology. This is evident in the following seven theological assertions that the authors of this document make without evidently realizing that each of them subordinates or replaces the Jewish religion:

1. The law (the torah) can reveal sin but it is unable to deal with sin:

   > The Law did not bring with it a remedy for sin for even if he [Paul] recognizes that the Law is good and wishes to keep it, the sinner is forced to declare, "For I do not do the good I want, but the evil I do not want is what I do" (Rom 7:19) . . . And sin produces death that provokes the sinner's cry of distress, "Wretched man that I am! Who will rescue me from this body of death?"(Rom 7:24). Thus is manifested the urgent need of redemption.[30]

2. Judaism is replaced as God's chosen people by a new nation, the church, which is the authentic continuation of Judaism.

---

28. Vatican Commission, *Guidelines*, sect. 3.

29. Vatican Commission, *Notes*, sect. 1 (emphasis mine).

30. Pontifical Biblical Commission, *Jewish People*, sect. 30.

At the conclusion of the parable of the murderous vine-yard tenants, addressed to the "chief priests" and "elders of the people" (Matt 21:33), Jesus says to them, "The kingdom of God will be taken away from you and given to a nation that will produce its fruit" (Matt 21:43). This word does not mean, however, the substitution of a pagan nation for the people of Israel. The new "nation" will be, on the contrary, in continuity with the chosen people, for it will have as a "cornerstone" the "stone rejected by the builders" (Matt 21:42) who is Jesus, a son of Israel, and it will be composed of Israelites with whom will be associated in "great numbers" (Matt 8:11) people coming from "all the nations"(Matt 28:19). The promise of God's presence with his people, which guaranteed Israel's election, is fulfilled by the presence of the risen Lord with his community.[31]

3. This new Israel is a "chosen remnant" of Jews who accepted Jesus. God's fidelity to Israel is manifested in the remnant that formed the "new" Israel.

To the question of whether the election of Israel remains valid, Paul gives two different answers; the first says that the branches have been cut off because of their refusal to believe (Rom 11:17, 20) but "a remnant remains, chosen by grace" (Rom 11:5). It cannot, therefore, be said that God has rejected his people" (Rom 11:1–2). Israel failed to attain what it was seeking. The elect (that is, the chosen remnant) attained it, but the rest were hardened (Rom 11:7).[32]

The New Testament never says that Israel has been rejected. . . . She [the Church] understands her own existence as a participation in the election of Israel and in a vocation that belongs in the first place to Israel, despite the fact that only a small number of Israelites accepted it.[33]

31. Pontifical Biblical Commission, *Jewish People*, sect. 35.
32. Pontifical Biblical Commission, *Jewish People*, sect. 36.
33. Pontifical Biblical Commission, *Jewish People*, sect. 36.

4. The true Israel is to be defined not according to the flesh (the Jewish race) but according to the spirit (the promise). The true offspring of Abraham are those who are identified with Christ.

> In Rom 3:12, Paul affirms unhesitatingly "the superiority of the Jews" . . . Nevertheless, Paul immediately adds that it is not enough to belong physically to Israel in order to rank among the "children of God." Before all else it is necessary to be "children of the promise" (Rom 9:6–8), which according to the apostle's thinking implies belonging in Christ Jesus in whom "every one of God's promises is a Yes" (2 Cor 1:20). According to the letter to the Galatians, the "offspring of Abraham" can only be one which is identified with Christ and those who belong to him (Gal 3:16, 29).[34]

5. God's covenant with the Jewish people is established on a new foundation, the person and work of Christ Jesus.

> God's covenant with his people in the writings of the New Testament is placed in a context of fulfillment, that is, in a fundamental progressive continuity . . . In the New Testament, the covenant is established on a new foundation, the person and work of Christ Jesus; the covenant relationship is deepened and broadened, opened to all through Christian faith.[35]

6. Christ is the end and fulfillment of the law, to which the law was leading the people of God.

> Continuity is underlined by affirming that Christ is the end and fulfillment to which the Law was leading the people of God (Gal 3:24). For many Jews the veil with which Moses covered his face remains over the Old

---

34. Pontifical Biblical Commission, *Jewish People*, sect. 36.

35. Pontifical Biblical Commission, *Jewish People*, sect. 41.

Testament (2 Cor 3:13, 5), thus preventing them from recognizing Christ's revelation there.[36]

> The letter to the Hebrews quotes *in extenso* the prophetic message of the "new covenant" and proclaims its fulfill-ment in Christ "meditator of the new covenant." It dem-onstrates the insufficiency of the cultic institutions of the "first covenant"; priesthood and sacrifices were incapable of overcoming the obstacle set by sins, and incapable of establishing an authentic mediation between God and his people. These institutions are now abrogated to make way for the sacrifice and priesthood of Christ (Heb 7:18–19).[37]

7. The Jews' refusal of faith in Christ places the Jewish people in a situation of disobedience.

> The Pauline letters, then, manifest a twofold conviction: the insufficiency of the legal covenant of Sinai, on the one hand, and on the other, the validity of the covenant-promise. . . . Their [the Jews'] refusal of faith in Christ places the Jewish people in a situation of disobedience, but they are still "loved" and promised God's mercy (cf. Rom 11:26–32).[38]

As we have seen, in all the official documents of the Catholic Church regarding Judaism, there is a genuine concern to reach out to the Jewish people and to move beyond previous teachings that fostered "contempt of the Jews." And yet we have also sadly noted that these efforts continue to be rooted in a theology that under-stands Christ and Christianity as the fulfillment, and therefore the replacement, of "the Old Testament"—a theology that identifies the Jews as "disobedient" to God's will for them.

A recent and poignantly telling example of how this theology of replacement can infect efforts to reach out in goodwill to Jews was the remarks that Pope Francis made in his public audience of August 11, 2021. Reflecting on Paul's teachings on Judaism,

36. Pontifical Biblical Commission, *Jewish People*, sect. 41.

37. Pontifical Biblical Commission, *Jewish People*, sect. 42.

38. Pontifical Biblical Commission, *Jewish People*, sect. 41.

the pope stated that the torah "does not give life" and that "those who seek life need to look to the promise and to its fulfillment in Christ."[39]

After the Pope's remarks set off a torrent of complaints from Jewish leaders around the world, John Allen, a highly regarded Vaticanologist and journalist, attempted to mollify the pope's remarks by observing that "while Pope Francis may not always express himself with the theological precision some might like, the idea that he's insensitive to Jews or unconcerned about their fate just doesn't hold water."[40]

The problem is that Francis *did indeed express himself with theological precision.* He precisely summed up what has been the teaching of the Catholic and all Christian churches for some two thousand years! His words point to the basis for Christian claims of supremacy over Judaism and all other religions: All effort to "seek life" and find the Divine are "fulfilled in Christ."

In trying to assuage the concern of the Jewish leaders about the Pope's remarks, Cardinal Kurt Koch, head of the Pontifical Council for Promoting Christian Unity, reminded them that Francis's words "must be considered within the overall framework of Pauline theology."[41] Evidently, the good Cardinal was unaware, just as the pope was, that Paul's understanding of Christ as the fulfillment of the torah is precisely the original problem!

I have no doubt about Francis's sincerity and genuine "concern about the fate of the Jews." But until he puts his theology where his heart is, he will have trouble convincing Jews that he can really mean what he says. Until Pope Francis, and Christians in general, are ready to critically qualify and reinterpret that statement about all other religions having to be "fulfilled" in Christ, Christians will continue to have the theological basis for claiming that Christianity supersedes Judaism. And that is the basis for contempt of the Jews.

39. Francis, "General Audience."

40. Allen, "Pope Gets Lucky as Trip Offers."

41. Allen, "Vatican Cardinal Tries to Heal."

Chapter 5

Did the First Christians Worship Jesus?

IN MY EFFORTS TO redeem Jesus' name, I found that I had to dare to ask the question, Is Jesus God? Jesus was not officially decreed to be God until the Council of Nicaea in 325. Once such a statement was made, I believe Jesus was dishonored. Moses is held in high honor by the Jewish people, yet he is never declared to be God, and that is what makes him great. He is a servant of God. He is the beloved of God. And he is honored and respected not only by Jews but by Christians and Moslems. That is what I want for Jesus, for the person known as Jesus of Nazareth.

These questions lead me to ask, Did the first Christians worship Jesus? To answer that question, I recall recent Vatican statements:

> Jesus was and always remained a Jew. . . . There is no doubt that he wished to submit himself to the law (Gal 4:4), that he was circumcised and presented in the Temple like any Jew of his time (Luke 2:21, 22–24), that he was trained in the law's observance. He extolled respect for it (cf. Matt 5:17–20), and invited obedience to it (Matt 8:4). The rhythm of his life was marked by observance of pilgrimages on great feasts, even from his infancy (Luke 2:41–50; John 2:13; 7:10). The importance of the cycle of Jewish

feasts has been frequently underlined in the Gospel of John (2:13; 5:1; 7:2, 10, 37; 10:22; 12:1; 13:1; 18:28; 19:42).[1]

If Jesus "was and always remained a Jew," he never could have thought of himself as God or deemed himself worthy of worship. He was a charismatic Jew who drew crowds to himself and to the God he worshiped. To this day, Jews recognize Jesus of Nazareth as one like themselves.

JEWS AND JESUS

Joseph Klausner[2] (1874–1958) was a Jewish historian and professor of Hebrew literature. In his book *Jesus of Nazareth*, he describes the Jewish environment in Galilee where Jesus lived and taught. His book places Jesus entirely within Judaism until his last breath.

Jules Isaac (1877–1963), a respected Jewish historian in France, is best known for his book, *Jesus and Israel*, published in 1947. Among Catholics he is well known because of his influential conversations with Pope John XXIII in 1960 in which he asked the pope to set up a subcommittee to examine Catholic teaching about Jews in preparation for the Second Vatican Council. This meeting resulted in the publication of the 1965 conciliar document *Nostra Aetate*. In proposition two of his book, Isaac wrote, "Jesus, the Jesus of the Gospels, only Son and incarnation of God for Christians, in his human lifetime was a Jew, a humble Jewish artisan. This is a fact of which no Christian has a right to be unaware."[3]

Martin Buber (1878–1965) was an Austrian Jewish and Israeli philosopher best known for his philosophy of dialogue. In 1951, he published *Two Types of Faith*. In the foreword he wrote that Jesus was his brother: "From my youth onwards I have found in Jesus my great brother . . . my own fraternal relationship to him has grown ever stronger and clearer, and to-day I see him more

1. Vatican Commission, *Notes*, sect. 3, 18–20.
2. Klausner, *Jesus of Nazareth*.
3. Isaac, *Jesus and Israel*, 11.

strongly and clearly than ever. I am more than ever certain that a great place belongs to him in Israel's history of faith."[4]

David Flusser, in the introduction to his book *Jesus*, wrote, "The present volume not only reflects that Jesus was a Jew and wanted to remain within the Jewish faith but argues that, without the long preparatory work of contemporaneous Jewish faith, the teachings of Jesus would be unthinkable."[5]

Amy-Jill Levine, in her book *The Misunderstood Jew*, wrote, "Jesus's earliest followers—Peter and Mary Magdalen, James and John, Joanna and Matthew—were, like Jesus himself, Jews. This designation signals not only their identification with the people of Israel but also their participation in a common set of practices and beliefs. Like Jesus, they honored the Torah and followed Mosaic law as they interpreted it."[6]

Yellow Crucifixion, by Marc Chagall, 1943

4. Buber, *Two Types of Faith*, 12–13.

5. Flusser, *Jesus*, 13.

6. Levine, *Misunderstood Jew*, 53.

Mark Chagall (1887–1985), a Jewish painter, presented Jesus as a faithful Jew. One of my favorite paintings is his *Yellow Crucifixion*. Jesus is crucified wearing his prayer shawl-loincloth and phylacteries (tefillin), which are donned by Jews for their liturgical prayers. Jesus' right arm is joined to the open Torah. He is one of the persecuted Jews who are trying to escape the Nazis.

When these Jewish writers and the church herself emphasize that Jesus was a faithful Jew, they are clearly implying that Jesus of Nazareth could never have been considered by his followers—nor by himself—to be God.

NEW TESTAMENT WRITERS

Now I turn to the writings of Paul and the Gospel writers and ask, Did the early Christians worship Jesus as God? By worship I mean the feeling or expression of reverence and adoration for a deity. I conclude with what a Christology might look like if Jesus is not portrayed as God.

Is Jesus God in the Epistles of Paul?

When reflecting on Paul's description of Jesus, we must begin with his experience of the resurrected Jesus that changed his orientation to life. He described that experience in simple, yet powerful, terms:

> It is no longer I who live, but it is Christ who lives in me. (Gal 2:20)

> Yet whatever gains I had, these I have come to regard as loss because of Christ. More than that, I regard everything as loss because of the surpassing value of knowing Christ Jesus my Lord. For his sake I have suffered the loss of all things, and I regard them as rubbish, in order that I may gain Christ. (Phil 3:7–8)

As far as we know, Paul did not meet the earthly Jesus. As noted in chapter 5, none of Paul's letters focus on the historical Jesus, which is a reason why the Jewish Jesus is basically ignored.

For Paul, Jesus Christ is the new Adam. In Christ a reversal of history occurred:

> Therefore, just as one man's trespass led to condemnation for all, so one man's act of righteousness leads to justification and life for all. For just as by the one man's disobedience the many were made sinners, so by the one man's obedience the many will be made righteous. (Rom 5:18–19)

> For since death came through a human being, the resurrection of the dead has also come through a human being; for as all die in Adam, so all will be made alive in Christ. (1 Cor 15:21–22)

According to Paul, the whole of humanity was implicated in Adam's disobedience. In Jesus' obedience, the trajectory of history was reversed. Not condemnation but justification. Not death but life. With the first Adam, humanity was infected with sin and faced a life of hopelessness, despair, and death. Through Jesus Christ, the second Adam, came acquittal, righteousness, and life (Rom 5:18–19). Where sin reigned, grace was poured out; where death ruled, life was promised: "For since death came through a human being, the resurrection of the dead has also come through a human being" (1 Cor 15:21–22).

Though Paul exalts Jesus, he exalts him as a human being.

- Therefore, just as one man's trespass led to condemnation for all, so one man's act of righteousness leads to justification and life for all.

- For just as by the one man's disobedience the many were made sinners, so by the one man's obedience the many will be made righteous.

- For since death came through a human being, the resurrection of the dead has also come through a human being.

Roger Haight comments,

> The comparison with Adam makes it clear that Jesus is a
> human being. This is not a pre-existence Christology, but
> a two-stage Christology in which the one compared with
> Adam is Jesus of Nazareth who went to his death in obe-
> dience, was raised and exalted, and is now the one who
> determines humanity into the end time. Jesus Christ, the
> human being, was the vehicle of God's action of love for
> humankind (Rom 5:8).[7]

As the vehicle of God's action, Paul's Christology is one of agency. God is God and Jesus is an agent of God. Christians did not hesitate to use Jewish titles for Jesus in their hymns—Sophia, Wisdom of God, Word of God. But such titles were never equated with a divine being.

> Ideas of "pre-existence" are to be read as extrapolations
> that spring from an experience of Jesus, and they have
> their basis in him . . . Descriptively these assertions are
> saying that in Jesus is embodied and therefore revealed
> the very wisdom of very God . . . It is mistaken to read
> this wisdom language as though it were straight-forward
> descriptive language that told the story of a divine being
> that descended to become Jesus.[8]

It is clear that Paul did not present Jesus as God. For Paul, Jesus is a powerful agent of God, but he is not God. Not only does Paul emphasize the humanness of Jesus but in several passages, he speaks of God as the "God and Father of our Lord Jesus Christ" (Rom 15:6; 2 Cor 1:3; Eph 1:3). The most common words for praise and thanksgiving are never offered to Christ but give thanks to God for what Jesus has done.

7. Haight, *Jesus*, 157.
8. Haight, *Jesus*, 171–72.

Is Jesus God in the Gospel According to Mark?

The answer Mark gives to the question of whether Jesus is God can be found in his opening sentence, "The beginning of the good news of Jesus Christ, the Son of God." These two titles, "Jesus Christ" and "Son of God," summarize the intent of the whole Gospel. "Son of God" interprets "Jesus Christ," and "Jesus Christ" interprets "Son of God." Thus, the Gospel has a thesis: Jesus is messiah (Christ) and Jesus is Son of God. "Son of God" indicates that Jesus is an agent of God, and "Jesus *Christ*" (the Greek word for messiah) specifies this agency.

Haight writes,

> The language Son of God indicates that Jesus is designated as God's agent; messiah further specifies this agency. People experienced or encountered God in Jesus. This experience overflows the person of Jesus, and the title Son of God draws its meaning from the experience that Jesus is empowered by God's *shekinah* or presence or dynamic power.[9]

That Jesus is Son of God, an agent of God, with a special mission as messiah is elaborated in four texts: Mark 1:11, 9:7; 14:61; 15:39.[10]

Mark 1:11: Jesus is coming up out of the water, having been baptized by John the Baptist. He sees the heavens torn open and the Holy Spirit descending upon him as a dove. He hears a voice that says, "You are my beloved Son; with you I am well pleased." This declaration is modeled upon Ps 2:7 where, to the newly enthroned king of Israel, God says, "You are my son; today I have begotten you." Just as the new king did not come about through inheritance or by his own action but by a direct action of God, so Jesus, a beloved son of Israel, is chosen as a special agent of God. Twice, Mark has the evil spirits recognize Jesus as Son of God (Mark 3:11) and they address Jesus as "Son of the Most High God" (Mark 5:7).

9. Haight, *Jesus*, 162.

10. Haight, *Jesus*, 160–63.

Mark 9:2–8: As Peter, James, and John look upon Jesus, his garments begin to glisten and become intensely white with the glory of God. He is standing between two of Israel's most important religious figures, Moses and Elijah. A cloud overshadows them and a voice comes out of the cloud, "This is my beloved Son—listen to him."

In this scene, Jesus is again presented as a beloved son, one with Moses and Elijah. With garments glistening and intensely white, he is a Moses figure, the skin of whose face is shining because he is talking with God (Exod 34:29). And like the prophet Elijah whose name means "Yah is my God," Jesus was called to be a prophet and seen as one like Elijah (Mark 6:15).

Mark 14:61: In the passion narrative, the high priest asks Jesus, "Are you the Christ [Messiah], the Son of the Blessed One?" In the linking of these two names, Jesus is again declared Son of God and Messiah. Haight asks,

> But what does this say about the status of the Son of God, since messiahship was a human office? In the context of the question of the high priest, "Son of God" connotes divine appointment rather than divine nature.[11]

Mark 15:39: "Now when the centurion, who stood facing him, saw that in this way he breathed his last, he said, 'Truly this man was God's Son!'" In this manner, Mark ends his Gospel with the same words as his opening. Jesus is Son of God and Messiah.

> Messiahship defines Jesus' status as Son of God in functional rather than metaphysical categories. It should not be considered in the sense it gained by the time of the patristic Christological debates.[12]

My conclusion is that for Mark, Jesus is a Son of God, not God. People experienced God in Jesus, as an agent of God, empowered by God to act.

11. Haight, *Jesus*, 161.

12. Haight, *Jesus*, 161.

Is Jesus God in the Gospel According to Matthew?

As I've noted in the previous chapter, the Gospel according to Matthew reveals different levels of composition, an early version that is pro-Jewish and later versions where the Jews are cast aside.[13] In the earlier version we come closer to the historical Jesus, who is described as a faithful Jew. As a faithful Jew he could not have allowed himself to be worshiped as God nor would his disciples have worshiped a human being, even if that person were Jesus of Nazareth.

> Do not think that I have come to abolish the law or the prophets; I have come not to abolish but to fulfill. For truly I tell you, until heaven and earth pass away, not one letter, not one stroke of a letter, will pass from the law until all is accomplished. Therefore, whoever breaks one of the least of these commandments, and teaches others to do the same, will be called least in the kingdom of heaven; but whoever does them and teaches them will be called great in the kingdom of heaven. (Matt 5:17–19)

That Jesus is a faithful Jew is supported with other texts within the Gospel. A lawyer asked Jesus which is the great commandment in the law (the torah). In reply, Jesus gave a synopsis of the whole torah:

> You shall love the Lord your God with all your heart and with all your soul and with all your mind. This is the great and first commandment. And a second is like it: You shall love your neighbor as yourself. On these two commandments depend all the Law and the Prophets. (Matt 22:37–40)

The first and greatest commandment to love God with one's whole heart, with all one's soul and with all one's mind, are the opening words of a prayer known as the Shema. Observant Jews consider the Shema, which they recite twice daily, to be the most important part of the prayer service in Judaism.

13. Cook, *Modern Jews*, 192–93.

The third verse of the Shema is a commandment to wear *tzitzit* (in Greek *kraspedon*, which is translated as fringe, edge, border, corner, and tassel) on the corners of their garments. Evidence exists that Jesus wore tassels on his garments. A woman who had suffered from a discharge of blood for twelve years came up behind him and touched the fringe of his garment and was healed.

Another important daily prayer in Judaism is the Amidah, an ancient prayer of eighteen benedictions, composed in the fifth century BCE. The Our Father is a shortened form of the Amidah. Of the Amidah, it was written: "In the first blessings one resembles a servant who praises his master, in the middle ones, one resembles a servant requesting some gift from his master, and in the last ones, one resembles a servant who has received his gift and takes his leave."[14] These three levels are contained in the Our Father.

Jesus said, "Pray, then, in this way:"

> Our Father in heaven,
> May your name be revered as holy.
> May your kingdom come,
> May your will be done,
> on earth as it is in heaven.
> Give us today our daily bread.
> And forgive us our debts,
> as we also have forgiven our debtors.
> And do not bring us to the time of trial,
> but rescue us from the evil one. (Matt 6:6–13)
> (For yours is the kingdom, and the power, and the glory forever.)

Still another example that Jesus and his followers were faithful Jews is their observance of the Sabbath. In Mark's Gospel, when Jesus and his disciples arrived in Capernaum on the Sabbath, they went immediately to the synagogue, and Jesus taught (1:21). In Luke, Jesus "came to Nazareth, where he had been brought up; and he went to the synagogue, as his custom was, on the Sabbath day" (4:16). And Matthew, knowing the laws surrounding travel on the

---

14. Donin, *To Pray as a Jew*, 73.

Sabbath, has Jesus say, "Pray that your flight may not be in winter or on a Sabbath" (24:20).

All of these examples proclaim that Jesus' disciples did not worship Jesus as God. As faithful Jews they could not worship anything in the likeness of God, even if that likeness was Jesus of Nazareth:

> Then God spoke all these words: "I am the LORD your God, who brought you out of the land of Egypt, out of the house of slavery. You shall not have other gods beside me. You shall not make for yourself an idol, whether in the form of anything that is in heaven above or that is on the earth beneath or that is in the water under the earth. You shall not bow down to them or serve them." (Exod 20:1–5)

It is evident from Matthew's Gospel that the early Christians had a clear memory that Jesus called for worship to be given only to God, and he himself regularly prayed to God as his God and Father.

Is Jesus God in the Gospel According to Luke?

To answer the question of whether or not Luke presented Jesus as God requires that we understood the power by which Jesus did what he did. Luke clearly recognizes that Jesus' extraordinary actions derived not from himself but from the Spirit of God.

Luke's Gospel has been labeled a Spirit Christology because the Jesus in this Gospel is conceived, anointed, and empowered by the Holy Spirit. It is the same Holy Spirit that is found in the Hebrew Scriptures and referred to as *Ruah HaKodesh* (Spirit of the Holy One) and *Ruah Elohim* (Spirit of God). The Holy Spirit is the power of God's Presence, also referred to as the "finger of God."

A number of examples point to the Holy Spirit active in Jesus' life from his conception to his death.

The Annunciation

> An angel appeared to Mary of Nazareth and said, "Greetings, favored one! The Lord is with you." But she was much perplexed by his words and pondered what sort of greeting this might be. The angel said to her, "Do not be afraid, Mary, for you have found favor with God. And now, you will conceive in your womb and bear a son, and you will name him Jesus . . . Mary said to the angel, "How can this be, since I am a virgin?" The angel said to her, "The Holy Spirit will come upon you, and the power of the Most High will overshadow you; therefore the child to be born will be holy; he will be called Son of God." (Luke 1:28–35)

The verbs "coming upon" and "overshadowing" are reminiscent of the Spirit of God that "hovered" over the abyss at creation (Gen 1:1–20). The word "hovered" is a biblical Hebrew word and refers to a dove hovering over its nest. When the Spirit of God hovered like a dove over the abyss, an exuberant world came slowly and steadily into existence. When the Spirit of God hovered over Mary, she conceived Jesus. This is the same Holy Spirit that was active when the barren women Sarah, Rebekah, and Rachel, and Elizabeth, an old woman beyond child-bearing age, became pregnant. This is the same Holy Spirit that anointed and empowered Jesus of Nazareth for his mission.

The Baptism of Jesus

> Now when all the people were baptized, and when Jesus also had been baptized and was praying, the heaven was opened, and the Holy Spirit descended upon him in bodily form like a dove. And a voice came from heaven, "You are my Son, the Beloved; with you I am well pleased." (Luke 3:21–22)

When Christians read, "You are my Son," one of the first thoughts that usually comes to mind is the second person of the Blessed

Trinity, "Son of God, true God from true God, begotten not made," etc. which is a doctrine established by the church during the Council of Nicaea in the fourth century. It often comes as a shock to Christians to learn that this was not at all the way "Son of God" was understood at the time of Jesus. In Jewish thinking, Son of God is read collectively of Israel: "Then you shall say to Pharaoh, 'Thus says the LORD, Israel is my firstborn son,' and I say to you, 'Let my son go that he may serve me'" (Exod 4:22). And in Romans: "For you did not receive the spirit of slavery to fall back into fear, but you have received the Spirit of adoption as sons, by whom we cry, 'Abba! Father!' The Spirit himself bears witness with our spirit that we are children of God" (8:15–16).

In the baptism scene, the Holy Spirit descended upon Jesus and commissioned him as an agent of God.

Then Jesus, "filled with the power of the Spirit," returned to Galilee (Luke 4:14). When he reached Nazareth, he went to the synagogue and was handed the scroll of the prophet Isaiah, and he began to read:

> The Spirit of the Lord is upon me because he has anointed me to bring good news to the poor. He has sent me to proclaim release to the captives and recovery of sight to the blind, to let the oppressed go free, to proclaim the year of the Lord's favor. (Luke 4:18–19)

Here we see more clearly a description of Jesus as an agent of God. In addition to these acts, Jesus, filled with the Holy Spirit, and empowered by the Holy Spirit, casts out demons.

Of note, Jesus does not cast outs demons by his own power but by the power of God:

> Now he was casting out a demon that was mute; when the demon had gone out, the one who had been mute spoke, and the crowds were amazed. But some of them said, "He casts out demons by Beelzebub, the ruler of the demons. . . . But he knew what they were thinking and said to them . . . Now if I cast out the demons by Beelzebub, by whom do your exorcists cast them out? But if it is

by the finger of God that I cast out the demons, then the
kingdom of God has come upon you. (Luke 11:14–20)

Here Jesus announces that he does not cast out demons by his
own power but by the power of God.

In Luke's Christology, Luke makes creative use of a familiar
symbol for God in Jewish tradition. The Holy Spirit in the Hebrew
Scriptures is God's active, creative, and prophetic presence in the
world and in God's people. For Luke, as for the Jews, the Spirit is a
metaphor that affirms that God is present in the world. The Holy
Spirit is no other than God manifesting the divine Self in nature
and human beings.

And it is this Spirit that, for Luke, originates, grounds, and
directs the entire life and ministry of Jesus. From the very first
moment of his existence, at his conception, it was the Spirit at
work through the cooperation and courageous faith of Mary. At
the launching of his ministry, his baptism, it is again the Spirit that
hovers over Jesus in the bodily form of a dove. And after Jesus'
retreat in the wilderness, which included the harrowing account of
his temptations, he sets forth on his ministry of healing and exor-
cism "in the power of the Spirit" (Luke 4:14). The active presence
of God gave authority to Jesus' teaching and enabled him to do
wondrous good works.

Clearly, Jesus is presented in Luke's Gospel as one empowered
by God. He didn't possess the power of God; the power of God
possessed him but in a manner that respected his free will. Jesus is
the ever ready and transparent vehicle and, therefore, revelation,
of the Spirit of God. For Luke, the revealer was never identified
with the revealed.

Is Jesus God in the Gospel According to John?

Many who read the prologue of John's Gospel (John 1:1–14) answer "yes" to the question, Is Jesus God in the Gospel according
to John? Their "yes" is supported by other statements in John's
Gospel: "Before Abraham was, I am" (John 8:58); "I and the Father

are one" (John 10:30); and, "If you've seen me, you've seen the Father" (John 14:9). These are statements found only in the Gospel of John. In earlier Gospels, including the writings of Paul, there is no indication that Jesus spoke these words. These are subsequent interpretations of who Jesus was for the Johannine community.

Yet no biblical text has had more influence on the development of Christology than the prologue of John's Gospel. The prologue is a key text for understanding the entire Gospel of John. It provides the basis for John's answer to whether or not Jesus is God.

> In the beginning was the Word, and the Word was with God, and the Word was God. He was in the beginning with God. All things came into being through him, and without him not one thing came into being . . . And the Word became flesh and lived among us, and we have seen his glory, the glory as of a father's only son, full of grace and truth. (John 1:13, 14)

These words have undergone multiple interpretations that can be divided into two streams: literal readings and metaphorical readings.

A Literal Reading

In a literal reading, a three-stage Christology of preexistence is implied, i.e., descent and ascent of a divine being. Jesus Christ, identified as the Word of God, was with God from the beginning. The Word of God descended and became flesh in Jesus of Nazareth, and after his death Jesus ascended to sit at the right hand of God and later was understood to be the second person of the blessed Trinity. In this interpretation, the Word of God that spoke to the prophets became personal in Jesus of Nazareth, as an independent subject and actor on earth.

This theology has close links with what is called wisdom Christology, which is based on the earlier Jewish image of Wisdom personified as a divine companion of God (Prov 8:22–31). In Phil 2:6–7, Jesus is an exalted companion of God who descended to earth and became incarnate:

who, though he was in the form of God, did not regard equality with God as something to be exploited, but emptied himself, taking the form of a slave, being born in human likeness. And being found in human form . . .

In Col 1:15–17, Jesus is

the image of the invisible God, the firstborn of all creation; for in him all things were created in heaven and on earth . . . all things were created through him and for him. He is before all things, and in him all things hold together.

In these quotations we perceive the language of Wisdom in the Hebrew Scriptures: "The Lord created me [Wisdom] at the beginning of his work" (Prov 8:22); "From eternity, in the beginning, he created me [Wisdom]" (Sir 24:9); "For she [Wisdom] is . . . an associate in his works" (Wis 8:4). We may ask, Are these texts telling us that God literally has a divine companion whose name is Wisdom? Not likely. Such a concept is totally foreign to the Jewish concept of the One God. Haight adds,

It is mistaken to read this wisdom language as though it were straight-forward descriptive language that told the story of a divine being that descended to become Jesus . . . Wisdom is not other than God, so that the action of God's wisdom is God acting very wisely.[15]

Yet here is a text in John's Gospel where a divine being, the Logos (the Word) or Sophia (Wisdom) descends and becomes incarnate in Jesus. The word of God that the prophets heard has become distinct and personal in Jesus and can be seen: "We have beheld his glory" (John 1:14). Before the birth of Jesus, the "word" of God was never portrayed as distinct and personal in any one person. So the question arises, How should we read the prologue of John's Gospel?

15. Haight, *Jesus*, 172–73.

A Metaphorical Reading

Different ways exist to express Truth. Myth is one of them. The mythical stories of creation are a way to proclaim that God is creator of the universe and how suffering, death, and evil came into the world. Metaphor is another way to express the truth. A metaphor is "a figure of speech" that describes an object or action in a way that isn't literally true, for example, "life is a roller coaster." Life isn't really a roller coaster but is a way of saying that life has many emotional ups and down similar to how roller coasters have physical ups and downs on their track.

"And the Word became flesh" is a metaphorical way of expressing the greatness of Jesus. Haight writes,

> These affirmations about the cosmic, extra-worldly-existence and behavior of the Logos [Word of God] are poetic and imaginative in the most profound sense. They are a means of expressing the significance and status of Christ in the personal lives of the Christian community.[16]

When the prologue is read metaphorically/poetically we can affirm a two stage Christology; that is, Jesus of Nazareth did not preexist before he was born of Mary.

Such a reading does not take from Jesus' greatness but adds to it: "The realism of incarnation in 'flesh' is meant to express dramatically the concrete visibility and availability of God's revelation in Jesus."[17]

When the prologue is read according to its genre, as a poem, a hymn of worship, it recalls the awesome claim not that Jesus is God, but that it is God who is encountered in Jesus, in the flesh, so that God is truly revealed in him.[18]

16. Haight, *Jesus*, 177.

17. Haight, *Jesus*, 177.

18. Haight, *Jesus*, 178.

CONCLUSION

In this chapter I examined the writings of Paul and the Gospels for an answer to the question, Did the first Christians worship Jesus? I've concluded that they did not.

Other New Testament scholars and historians agree. James Dunn wrote,

> So when we transpose our findings into an answer to our central question, the dominant answer for Christian worship seems to be that the first Christians did not think of Jesus to be worshipped in and for himself . . . and the corollary is that, in an important sense, Christian monotheism, if it is to be truly monotheism, has still to assert that only God, only the one God, is to be worshipped.[19]

The early followers of Jesus could not have forgotten that Jesus of Nazareth forbade worship of any other than God, and that he prayed to God as an expression of his own need and reliance on God.[20]

Dunn warned that Christian worship could deteriorate into what may be called Jesus-olatry. What he means is very close to the meaning of the word idolatry. In idol worship, the worship due to God is absorbed by the idol. The danger of Jesus-olatry is that Jesus is substituted for God, that the worship due to God is absorbed in him.[21] The worship that constitutes Christianity is the worship of God enabled by Jesus. The only one to be worshiped is the One God.[22]

Geza Vermes, a New Testament historian wrote,

> None of the Synoptic Gospels try to do this [equate Jesus with God]. Indeed, it is no exaggeration to contend that the identification of a contemporary historical figure with God would have been inconceivable to a first-century Jew . . . Paul, the Jew from Tarsus, at home in the

19. Dunn, *First Christians*, 146.
20. Dunn, *First Christians*, 145.
21. Dunn, *First Christians*, 147.
22. Dunn, *First Christians*, 150, 151.

Greco-Roman world, shies away from it. Even the theologizing author of the Fourth Gospel, writing a couple of generations later, shows understandable diffidence . . . It was not until Gentiles began to preach the Jewish Gospel to the Hellenized peoples of the Roman empire that the hesitation disappeared and the linguistic brake was lifted . . . When Christianity later set out to define the meaning of *son of God* in its creed, the paraphrase it produced—"God of God, Light of Light, true God of true God, consubstantial with the Father"—drew its inspiration, not from the pure language and teaching of the Galilean Jesus, nor even from Paul the Diaspora Jew, but from a Gentile-Christian interpretation of the Gospel adapted to the mind of the totally alien world of pagan Hellenism.[23]

A Christology for Today

If Jesus is not God, how might we approach Christology today? Roger Haight divides the different Christologies in the New Testament into two main streams: Logos (Word) Christology and Spirit Christology. Logos Christology has been understood as beginning "from above" and has its source in the prologue of John's Gospel. Spirit Christology, found primarily in Luke's Gospel, begins "from below." Logos Christology "from above" has been the dominant Christology in the Christian churches since earliest times and is still dominant today.

Spirit Christology is focused from below on the experience of Jesus, on the empowerment of Jesus by the Holy Spirit. The Holy Spirit, viewed as identical with God and not other than God, points to God as immanent; it is the same Spirit of God referred to in Ps 139:7, "Where can I go from your spirit or where can I flee from your presence?"

Logos Christology, when viewed "from below," is not a Christology in which Jesus descended from above to earth; rather, he became the Word of God through the power of the Holy Spirit.

23. Vermes, *Jesus the Jew*, 212–13.

As he became the Word of God, those who approached him sensed the nearness and the visibility of God, as did those who approached Moses at Sinai.

When read in this manner, Christology is truly incarnational. Jesus embodied God's wisdom; Jesus was the Word of God symbolically because he embodied God's word to Israel and to the Johannine community.

When Logos Christology and Spirit Christology are combined, we have a model image of how to become, like Jesus, an enfleshed word of God. For the combining to take place, Logos Christology must be recast in the framework of a Christology from below—Jesus becomes the Word of God through the empowerment of the Holy Spirit. In such a Christology, Jesus is truly the embodiment of the Divine, but not necessarily the only such embodiment. Christians are invited to be open to other symbolic actualizations of God's loving presence to humankind. "More" of God can be revealed if Jesus is not the only way to the Father. God is free to approach humankind in a variety of ways and in more than one medium.[24]

These new teachings witness to an incipient Copernican revolution in church teaching that has still to be carried out in its fullness. As these teachings on the irrevocability of the covenant with Israel and on the Jewishness of Jesus are taught, preached, and implemented, the church will finally be able to recognize, repent of, and move beyond its sordid history of provoking or supporting anti-Semitism. And doors of dialogue between Christians and Jews will open.

These possibilities of dialogue will extend beyond Judaism and will facilitate dialogue and collaboration not only between religions but also between nations and ethnic groups. Dialogue, which is a vital instrument for all forms of peacemaking, is only possible when the dialogue takes place on an equal playing field on which all share equal dignity and rights. Claims of supremacy or superiority—of being innately, inherently superior over all others—are both an obstacle to peacemaking and a cause of violence.

24. Haight, *Jesus*, 431–39.

And such claims of supremacy—whether they are racial, or national, or ethnic, or gendered—are generally inspired by, or justified by, claims of religious supremacy. Christians have traditionally affirmed that God has established Jesus as the only savior and therefore Christianity as the religion meant to replace—or nowadays we say fulfill—all other religions. On such a basis, interreligious relationships, though inspired by fervent calls for mutual dialogue and cooperation are, in the final analysis, a zero-sum game. If my religious truth or my Bible or my Qur'an—or my Savior, my Prophet, my Teacher—is supreme, then yours is not.

If Christians can deconstruct their long-time traditional claims to supersede Judaism, and if they can reconstruct a pluralistic theology that will recognize the validity of Judaism and other religions, they will provide an incentive toward building a world in which no nation will claim superiority over others and all nations will recognize their need to learn from each other.[25]

25. Knitter, *Jesus and the Other Names*, 23–45.

Chapter 6

Who Is Jesus for Me?

The New Testament scholar and Lutheran bishop Krister Stendahl urges us to find ways to sing our song about Jesus so that others can hear it, but to sing our song in such a way that does not put down or seek to replace the songs that others sing about Moses, or Buddha, or Krishna, or Mohammad.[1]

In this chapter I want to sing my song about Jesus so that others can hear but to sing it in a way that does not put down or seek to replace the songs of other great religions, especially the song of the Jews.

Though I have been describing who Jesus is throughout this book, I want to sum up what I have written and state more clearly who Jesus is for me. In my relationship with Jesus, as is true of all my relationships, continued contact corrects false interpretations and reveals new aspects. What has become clear to me as I have deepened my relationship with Jesus in the context of ongoing experiences of my life is that the oft-quoted text that proclaims Jesus as the only way to the Father must not be read literally (John 14:6). If Jesus is experienced and proclaimed as a true, definite way to the Holy Mystery he called "Father," then he cannot be the only way. A *true* way to the Father cannot be an *only* way, for the Father that

1. Stendahl, *Meanings*, 233; see also Knitter, "Christianity and the Religions," 5–17.

Jesus experienced is a God who loves all peoples and seeks to bring all people to the fullness of truth.

I have never been able to understand the mystery of the doctrine of the Trinity. I learned from the creation story that we are all part of God, made in the image and likeness of God, but not God. The first Christians did not worship Jesus as God, nor could Jesus have looked upon himself as God (chapter 5). That Jesus is God was formulated by a church council in the city of Chalcedon in 451. It is known as the Chalcedonian Creed and has been taken as the standard, orthodox definition of the biblical teaching on the person of Christ since that day by all the major branches of Christianity. It is well to recall that its teachings were brought about because of the number of contradictory teachings that were circulating at the time on the resurrected Jesus. The declarations of the Council of Chalcedon represent an attempt to state, in the philosophical concepts of the time, what it meant to confess Jesus as both human and divine. Admittedly, what made sense in the philosophical views of the world at that time may not speak to the views of our time. The councils of the church, like the Bible, must constantly be reinterpreted.

In what follows, what I say about Jesus is based on the following principles:

a. "Jesus was and always remained a Jew. He was fully a man of his time and of his environment—first century Jewish Palestine."[2]

b. The New Testament, especially the four Gospels, is a book of reflections on the historical Jesus based on experiences of the risen Jesus. Formal Christological interpretations began in the context of the early community's conviction that Jesus had risen. In their experience of the resurrected Jesus, they applied new titles to him, e.g., the new Adam, the Son of God, the Word of God incarnate, etc.[3]

2. Vatican Commission, *Notes*, sect. 3, 20.

3. Haight, *Jesus*, 180.

c. Different Christologies are presented in the New Testament. The source of these Christologies is the worshiping community. Jesus was interpreted from within the context of the specific traditions and languages of the various communities to whom he was introduced, thereby producing of necessity different understandings of Jesus. That is to say, the development of Christology did not happen, necessarily or exclusively, by way of inference from Jesus' teaching and sayings. The cultic veneration of Jesus in early Christian circles is the most important context for development of Christological titles and concepts.[4]

Because the nativity stories in Matthew and Luke are theological statements, not based on historical evidence, I present an interpretation that leaves Jesus more human and, I believe, more worthy of honor than do the traditional interpretations. I begin with reflections on his mother.

JESUS' MOTHER

In reflecting on who Jesus is for me, I begin with Mary his mother, though little is written about her in the Gospels. Matthew and Luke are the only Gospels with nativity stories, and Mark and John barely mention Mary. These Gospels were written many years after the death of Jesus, Matthew around 85 CE (likely in Antioch), and Luke around 94 CE (likely in Greece). And they differ in many respects. Raymond Brown, a noted Roman Catholic New Testament scholar, wrote that the nativity stories of Matthew and Luke are late editions to the Gospels and are theological statements rather than historical facts.[5] They were written backward from the oldest Christian preaching on the death and resurrection of Jesus.

And John Meier, another New Testament scholar, wrote,

> The historian must be wary about using the Infancy Narratives as sources for historical information about

4. Haight, *Jesus*, 180.

5. Brown, *Birth of the Messiah*, 26–38.

Jesus. Both narratives seem to be largely products of early Christian reflection on the salvific meaning of Jesus Christ in the light of OT Prophecies.[6]

The Roman Catholic Church built its own images of Mary from these Gospel accounts, which we find in official ecclesial statements such as the following:

- Council of Nicaea, 325: Mary was declared a virgin, before, during, and after the birth of Christ.

- First Council of Ephesus, 431: Mary was declared the mother of God.

- Pope Pius IX, in 1854, declared the doctrine of the Immaculate Conception, that God preserved the Virgin Mary from the taint of original sin from the moment she was conceived.

- Pope Pius XII, in 1950, declared that the Virgin Mary "having completed the course of her earthly life, was assumed body and soul into heavenly glory."[7]

Marina Warner, in her book *Alone of All Her Sex*,[8] gives lengthy descriptions of the titles and roles bestowed on Mary through official dogma, folk legend, art, history, literature, and psychology. She demonstrates that for all their beauty and power, and because of them, the legends of Mary have condemned real women to perpetual inferiority.

Professor Eamon Duffy, a specialist in the history of Christianity, wrote that the cult of Mary, for all its beauty, had been, on the whole, a damaging thing:

> Damaging above all for women, for in the Church's idealization of Mary, womanhood had been denigrated, not exalted. Mary, alone of all her sex, had pleased the Lord. The Church had been unable to cope with femininity. Woman was Eve, temptress and harlot, and only Mary, pure Virgin and perfect Mother, had escaped the blight

6. Meier, *Marginal Jew*, 213.

7. Pius XII, *Munificentissimus*.

8. Warner, *Alone of All Her Sex*.

of Eve. As a model for women, she doomed them to be either sexless daughters or sexlessly maternal, thereby emptying the Christian world-view of any convincing place for female sexuality and more generally for eroticism, and reducing the likelihood of real and equal sexual relations between men and women.[9]

With these texts in mind, I looked anew at the infancy narratives. First, to be with child from the Holy Spirit (Luke 1:35) is not a sign that Jesus had no father. The Holy Spirit enabled married barren women become pregnant, e.g., Sarah (Gen 17:15–17), Rebekah (Gen 25:21), and Rachel (Gen 30:22). And in the New Testament, Zechariah and Elizabeth had no child. Elizabeth was barren. Both she and Zechariah were of an advanced age when an angel appeared to Zechariah while he was serving in the temple and said, "Do not be afraid, Zechariah, for your prayer has been heard, and your wife Elizabeth will bear you a son, and you shall call his name John" (Luke 1:13).

In Matt 1:16, "Joseph the husband of Mary, of whom Jesus was born" indicates that Joseph was the father of Jesus. But another text clearly states that he was not:

> Now the birth of Jesus the Messiah took place in this way. When his mother Mary had been engaged to Joseph, but before they lived together, she was found to be with child from the Holy Spirit.
>
> Her husband Joseph, being a righteous man and unwilling to expose her to public disgrace, planned to dismiss her quietly. (Matt 1:18–19)

Granting that every conception needs both a mother and a father, if Joseph is not Jesus' father, then who is? Jane Schaberg (1938–2012), an American biblical scholar, wrote that even though the "unnameable" is avoided, "evidence exists of a suspicion of rape."[10] On the basis of a broader analysis, she concludes that a

---

9. Duffy, *Madonnas That Maim?*.

10. Schaberg, *Illegitimacy of Jesus*, 251.

pre-gospel tradition about the illegitimacy of Jesus is probably grounded in historical memory.[11]

She asks why Matthew places the four questionable women—Tamar, Rahab, Ruth, and Bathsheba—beside Mary in his genealogy of Jesus (Matt 1:3–6). She argues that mention of these four is designed to lead Matthew's reader to expect another story of a woman who becomes a social misfit in some way, who is wronged or thwarted and who is party to a sexual act that places her in great danger, but whose story has an outcome that is uplifting.[12]

At the time of Jesus' conception, the country was occupied by Rome. Numerous Jewish women were raped by Roman soldiers. Could Mary have been one of them? Could she be identified with such women! Could Jesus be one of these children! Why does the Magnificat begin with these words, "And Mary said, 'My soul magnifies the Lord, and my spirit rejoices in God my Savior, for he has looked with favor on the *lowliness* of his servant'" (Luke 1:46–48, my emphasis). "The Greek term *tapeinosis* (low estate) regularly suggests positive humiliation and distress . . . In her Magnificat, Mary speaks as a prophet of the poor. She represents the hope of the poor, but she represents that hope of the poor as a woman who has suffered and been vindicated."[13]

After struggling in anguish with different descriptions of the conception and birth of Jesus, I had a dream where I approached Mary and asked her, "Mary, were you raped as a young woman?"

Mary replied, "Don't be afraid to ask questions. Questions lead to truth. I do not like being referred to as flawless, as perfect. Perfection is static. Those who are perfect are incapable of change or growth.

"Since you want to know, let me tell you my story. I was born in Nazareth of Jewish parents. Like other teenage girls my age I was a shepherdess, and I led the sheep and goats to pasture every day. I loved it—the rain in winter enlivening the dry earth, the multiple flowers that carpeted the fields in the spring, and wildlife scurrying

11. Schaberg, *Illegitimacy of Jesus*, 251.

12. Schaberg, *Illegitimacy of Jesus*, 247.

13. Schaberg, *Illegitimacy of Jesus*, 94–96.

here and there. I talked to the sheep and the goats. I had names for each of them. But one day when I was lying in the grass looking up at the bright, cloudless, blue sky singing softly to myself, a dark shadow passed over me. Someone grabbed me. I struggled to get free. Then a blow and I must have gone unconscious. When I came to, my clothes were ripped and stained with blood. I was sore between my legs. I began to cry and sob into the grass.

"As evening was drawing near, I went home with the flock. I slipped quietly away and changed my clothes. Terrified, I decided to tell no one what happened, not even Joseph, my fiancé.

Erre, 2010

"A month later I suspected I was pregnant. When my periods ended, I became frantic. One day, about the third month, I saw Joseph looking at me in a strange way. When he left, I hid and I cried and begged God to please tell me what to do. As I sat mourning, I heard a dove flapping its wings on my windowsill. It seemed to be talking to me. I heard a Voice, but not with my ears, 'You have a son within your womb; you shall call his name Jesus. He will be great and will be called the Son of the Most High.' With these words an ocean of peace enveloped me. Suddenly I wanted this child.

"The next day I was ready to tell my family. Though at peace, I couldn't keep back the tears as I told them what happened. I wept and wept. We knew that with the stigma of rape upon me, it would now be exceedingly difficult for Joseph to marry me. While I was weeping Joseph entered our dwelling. He came forward and clasped me in his arms and said, "I learned that you were pregnant, and I knew I would have to divorce you. But as I considered these things behold, an angel of the Lord appeared to me in a dream, saying, "Joseph, son of David, do not fear to take Mary as your wife, for that which is conceived in her is from the Holy Spirit. She will bear a son, and you shall call his name Jesus, 'for he will save his people from their sins'" (Matt 1:20–21).

When I awoke, I was filled with a deep feeling of peace, though I knew that as with other presentations of Jesus' conception and birth, no historical evidence existed to support what I dreamt. I continued to wonder if a child conceived in this manner could be Jesus of Nazareth, Son of God, conceived by the Holy Spirit. And if every child, conceived and born in the same manner, could be a true son or daughter of God and rise to heroic heights as a mature person of wisdom and holiness. The answer I've come to is yes. Every child is born in the image and likeness of God, born with free will, with the ability to choose life.

Mary Transformed, by Doris Klein, 2016

If this narrative of Jesus' conception and birth has any weight, it opens the door for the recognition of all children, no matter what their historical or socioeconomic circumstances, as uniquely beloved of God. And for me, Jesus rises higher in my estimation of who he is. As does Mary his mother. Every woman can sing the Magnificat with Mary:

My soul magnifies the Lord, and my spirit rejoices in God my Savior, for he has looked with favor on the lowliness of his servant. Surely from now on all generations will call me blessed, for the Mighty One has done great things for me, and holy is his name. (Luke 1:46–49)

JESUS IS DIVINE

Then the Lord *God formed man from the dust of the ground, and breathed into his nostrils the breath of life; and the man became a living being.* (Gen 2:7)

In this section I focus on the divinity of Jesus. In previous chapters, I wrote that the early Christians did not worship Jesus as God. Jesus was a faithful Jew and could not have looked upon himself as God. This does not mean that he was not divine.

In pursuing my study of Jesus as divine, I begin with the story of the creation of Adam, who at first was nothing but a clod of earth. When God "breathed into his nostrils the breath of life; the man became a living creature" (Gen 2:7), God from God, Light from Light, true God from true God.

Jews in their daily morning service pray, "O my God, the soul that you gave me is pure; you did create it, you did form it, you did breathe it into me . . . and you will take it from me, and restore it to me in the future." The body and the soul are distinguished from each other. When the body dies, the soul departs.

Jewish mystics focus on five different names for soul found in the Bible: *nephesh* (Gen 1:20, 21, 24, 30), *ruah* (Gen 6:17; 7:15, 22); *neshamah* (Isa 2:22; 42:5; Ps 130:6), *hayyah* (together with *nephesh*, Gen 1:20, 24; 2:7), and *yehidah*[14] (Ps 22:21; 35:17). *Nephesh* is the lowest level, and the *yehidah* is the innermost, deepest level of the soul, which is a divine spark from God, an actual portion of God:

14. Jacobs, *On Ecstasy*, 66n9: "The *yehidah,* the highest stage of the divine soul, attaches itself to God as 'part' of God. The word *yehidah* is connected with the Hebrew word for 'attachment'—*yahad* = 'together.'"

> You are endowed from birth with a divine soul. This divine point, the *nekudah* [the *yehidah*], is infinite smallness that is infinite vastness, a limitless oneness that contains all the world within for it is bound and at one with its Source. But the point is hidden, and we have to expand it. This is the meaning of "When YHWH your God widens your border" (Deut 12:20)—when the point spreads forth and expands throughout the human soul.[15]

The Lubavitcher rabbi, Menachem M. Schneerson, referring to the divine soul, wrote,

> You are a plot of land (Mal 3:12) earthy, rough, but replete with potential treasure. Beneath the surface are wellsprings of life-giving waters, reserves of energy, and stores of precious metals and gems. Your soil is alive with the promise of lush crops, ready to sprout forth upon a proper investment of devoted toil.[16]

Christian writers refer to the same reality with other images. Theresa of Avila, for example, a Spanish mystic of the sixteenth century, described the soul as a most beautiful crystal globe, made in the shape of a castle, and containing seven mansions, in the seventh and innermost of which is God, in the greatest splendor, illuminating and beautifying them all.[17]

I had my own experience of God within me. I was in the early months of training to be a member of the Sisters of Sion. Our novice mistress suggested that we novices try to keep our hearts with Jesus on the altar (it was a time when the monstrance, a vessel containing the consecrated host, was displayed on the altar). Interpreting what she said literally, and with the enthusiasm and zeal of youth, I imagined my heart on the altar in the Chapel while I swept the floors and washed the windows in the school's classrooms. Stumbling over chairs and exhausted with the mental gymnastics that this demanded, I heard a Voice, not verbally, that said, "Why do you search for me there? I am within you."

15. Jacobs, *On Ecstasy*, 66.

16. Chabad, "Human Potential."

17. Avila, "Interior Castle," 187–351.

Astonished and overwhelmed, I dropped the broom and ran to my novice mistress. "Does God dwell within me?" I asked. "Yes, of course," she replied. Her answer seemed to be too matter of fact for the experience I had, so I demanded, "Really, in me? Really, really, in me?" She took a book from her library and handed it to me—a book with the title *God Within*, by Pere Plus.[18] I fairly danced out of her office, holding the book to my heart. I devoured it. I wasn't the same after that. If God was in me, God was in others, as well. We were all tabernacles of God with direct contact with God, empowered to become holy ones of God.

Years later, I came across a passage from the Catholic theologian Karl Rahner that both affirmed and clarified my early experience:

> The presence of God and the human person to each other is so intermingled that in one way or other both remain indestructible and interdependent, (although) the very obscurity of the presence of each in the other means that they can appear to be separated.[19]

God from God, Light from Light, true God from true God: These terms describe Jesus. The *nekudah* of "infinite smallness that is infinite vastness," expanded throughout the "human soul" of Jesus through the decisions he made. As the divine spark expanded, Jesus became godlike, and became known as the Holy One of God (but not God).

Once, when Jesus was in the synagogue in Nazareth, a man with the spirit of an unclean demon cried out in a loud voice, "I know who you are, the Holy One of God" (Luke 4:33). At another time, when Jesus was in Capernaum, some of his disciple disputed what Jesus was saying and left him. "Turning to the Twelve, Jesus asked, 'Do you want to go away as well?' Peter responded, 'Lord, to whom shall we go? You have the words of eternal life, and we have believed, and have come to know, that you are the Holy One of God'" (John 6:67–69).

18. Plus, *God within Us*.

19. Rahner, "Concerning the Relationship," 234.

In this manner of speaking, we can address Jesus in the words of the Council of Nicaea, "God from God, Light from Light, true God of true God"—but this does not mean that he is God, for to say that he is "God *from* God" signifies that he is from God, a divine spark, a portion of God, implanted within him at conception.

JESUS THE PROPHET

In my reflection on Jesus the prophet, I begin with statements from Moses and Soloveitchik who say that we are all called to be prophets. With those words, I will try to understand what it means to be a prophet. This will help me to better understand Luke's statement that Jesus of Nazareth was, "a prophet mighty in deed and word before God and all the people" (24:19).

When a young man ran to Moses and complained that Eldad and Medad were prophesying, Moses responded, "Are you jealous for my sake? Would that all the Lord's people were prophets, that the Lord would put his Spirit on them!" (Num 11:29).

Soloveitchik, a modern orthodox Jew, emphasized this teaching:

> Each person of whatever rank is called to be a prophet. One is not born a prophet. One becomes a prophet through one's own self-creation, through being faithful to one's own deeper self, which is empowered by the ever-abiding presence of God. The principle of prophesy has a twofold aspect: that God causes us to prophecy and that prophecy is a norm to which all are called to aspire to.[20]

Called to Be a Prophet

According to these words, life is our living Scripture. We become prophets through our own self creation, an outcome of our fidelity to our own deeper self. Fidelity to our deeper self is fidelity to

20. Soloveitchik, *Halakhic Man*, 128.

the divine urges coming from the abiding presence of God. These divine urges accompany us in our daily lives:

> God's address to us penetrates the events in all our lives and all the events in the world around us, everything biographical and everything historical. . . . Event upon event, situation upon situation is enabled and empowered by this personal language to call upon the human person to endure and decide.[21]

Buber continues that this word of God that addresses us now, not just sometimes, but in every now and in every here, is a personal word, not to be found in a guide or holy book. We are called to respond to the moment, as best we can. Nothing can relieve us of this responsibility, not the decisions of the group nor the church. But it does not mean that the group to which we belong does not concern us greatly; indeed, we must remain in ongoing dialogue with our community and be open to hearing the comments and critique of our community. But in the final analysis, only one thing matters: to be faithful to the moment and take what feels to be the next right step. It is the only certainty we have, and even that certainty remains an uncertain certainty.[22] We will make mistakes, which often proves to be an advantage. Our failures are some of our best teachers.

"To be" is a question of decision-making, fidelity to the divine urges within one. On a daily basis we are confronted with choices to make. Everything can be taken from us except our ability to choose. Victor Frankl questions whether a person in a Nazi prison camp is really free to make one's own decisions. He responds,

> The experiences of camp life show that the person does have a choice of action. There are enough examples, often of a heroic nature, which proved that apathy could be overcome, irritability suppressed. The person can preserve a vestige of spiritual freedom, of independence of mind, even in such terrible conditions of psychic and physical stress. We who lived in concentration camps can

21. Buber, *I and Thou*, 182.
22. Frankl, *Man's Search*, 68–69.

remember those who walked through the huts comforting others, giving away their last piece of bread. They may have been few in number, but they offer sufficient proof that everything can be taken from a person but one thing; the last of the human freedoms, to choose one's own way.

And there were always choices to make. Every day, every hour, offered the opportunity to make a decision, a decision which determined whether you would or would not submit to those powers which threatened to rob you of your very self, your inner freedom; which determined whether or not you would become the plaything of circumstance, renouncing freedom and dignity to become molded into the form of the typical inmate. . . . Few can attain this level of heroism. But it does witness that we can turn our inner life into an inner triumph or ignore the challenge and vegetate.[23]

In the words of the poet Richard Lovelace, "Stone walls did not a prison make, nor iron bars a cage."[24]

Jesus the Prophet

As Luke tells us, Jesus was "a prophet mighty in deed and word before God and all the people" (Luke 24:19). In Matthew's Gospel opponents sought to arrest Jesus, but they feared the crowds, for "they held him to be a prophet" (Matt 21:47); in Mark's Gospel he is one of the prophets of old (Mark 6:15); in Luke's Gospel, the people proclaimed, "A great prophet has arisen among us" (Luke 7:16); and in John's Gospel the people cried out, "This is indeed the prophet who is to come into the world" (John 6:14).

Jesus was not born a prophet. Along with other prophets, he became a prophet through his own self-creation, through being faithful to his own deeper self, which was empowered by the ever abiding presence of God. He told his disciples, "My food is to do the will of him who sent me and to accomplish his work" (John 4:34).

23. Frankl, *Man's Search*, 65.

24. Lovelace, "To Althea, from Prison."

He lived what he taught. He became, "a prophet mighty in deed and word before God and all the people" (Luke 24:19).

JESUS AND THE KINGDOM OF GOD

The orientation of Jesus' life was the kingdom of God. He taught his disciples,

> Pray then like this:
> Our Father in heaven,
> hallowed be your name.
> Your kingdom come,
> your will be done,
> on earth as it is in heaven. (Matt 6:9–10)

> The phrase "the kingdom of God" appears in more than thirty places in Luke's Gospel. That phrase describes the distinguishing feature and mission of Jesus—the reign of God. This reign was not just for the life to come in the next world or only for the spiritual needs of this world. The kingdom of God, the kingdom of heaven, stands for a mended creation with people and things—a social, economic, ecological reality. The kingdom with its justice is for the wronged and the oppressed; the little people who hunger and thirst for bread and for justice; the peacemakers who are so easily liquidated.[25]

To this end, Jesus healed the sick and fed the hungry. He ate with sinners. When a woman caught in adultery was about to be stoned to death, he saved her. His life was one of reaching out to those who were marginalized.

He needed help to build the kingdom. He chose twelve apostles. As he was walking around the Sea of Galilee, he saw peasant fishermen and said, "Come and join me." They left their nets and followed him. He met a tax collector near Capernaum, and he said, "Follow me." He followed him.

Then he began to teach them,

25. Knitter, "Christianity and the Religions," 20.

> You are the salt of the earth, but if salt has lost its taste,
> how shall its saltiness be restored? It is no longer good for
> anything except to be thrown out and trampled under
> people's feet.
>
> You are the light of the world. A city set on a hill
> cannot be hidden. Nor do people light a lamp and put it
> under a basket, but on a stand, and it gives light to all in
> the house.
>
> In the same way, let your light shine before others,
> so that they may see your good works and give glory to
> your Father who is in heaven. (Matt 5:13–16)

These ordinary folk are the ones Jesus wants on his team. He begins by praising them. They are salt of the earth. They are to let their light shine so that others may see their good works and give glory not to themselves, but to their Father who is in heaven. Salt, even in small dosages, makes a big difference in the taste of food. It adds taste and enhances its flavor. In the process of seasoning, the salt disappears and dissolves while giving its seasoning power to the food. Likewise with light. Light itself is invisible. Only with light do we see. Thus, both salt and light are mediums of a greater good, the building of the kingdom of God on earth.

Jesus' actions were accompanied by his teachings throughout Galilee and Judea. He proclaimed God's love for all people and the need for all people to love their enemies, not to fight violence with violence but with compassion.

> But love your enemies and do good, and lend, expect-
> ing nothing in return, and your reward will be great, and
> you will be sons of the Most High, for he is kind to the
> ungrateful and the evil. (Luke 6:35)

These words have an additional element in the Gospel according to Matthew:

> But I say to you, "Love your enemies and pray for those
> who persecute you, so that you may be children of your
> Father in heaven; for he makes his sun rise on the evil
> and on the good, and sends rain on the righteous and on
> the unrighteous." (Matt 5:44–45)

These are challenging statements for me—how, for example, do I forgive and love someone who has deceived and maligned me? But deceiving and maligning are pinpricks compared to those called to find a way to love murderers and abusers. Jesus, hanging torturously on the cross, looked down upon those who crucified him, and said, "Father, forgive them, for they know not what they do" (Luke 23:34).

Etty Hillesum, in the Westerbork concentration camp, which was the last stop before Auschwitz, where she was murdered, was able to stand before a Nazi, greet him and smile, as though he were an honorable man. Few Nazis knew what to do with such an approach—their power was threatened. In her diaries, Etty wrote that everyone who hates probably has a good reason to do so. But why, she asked, choose the cheapest and easiest way? In her view, every atom of hatred added to the world makes it an even more inhospitable place.[26]

She was exterminated in Auschwitz, but her words live on. I live in Jerusalem, in the midst of the Israeli–Palestinian conflict, where the method of resolution to the conflict is violence against violence. On a panel of speakers, I suggested the only road to the resolution of this conflict are the words of Jesus, "Love your enemies and do good, and lend, expecting nothing in return." From the reaction in the crowd, I felt the majority thought I was foolish and naïve.

Micah Goodman, in his book *Catch-67*, wrote that the clash between the Israelis and Palestinians is a clash of emotions. The dominant emotion among Israelis is fear of the Palestinians. The dominant emotion among Palestinians is humiliation. These emotions nurture and aggravate each other. The Israelis' fear of Palestinians pushes them to take defensive steps such as placing restrictions on Palestinian movement, delaying their passage through checkpoints, and questioning them at the entrance to public places. The Palestinian sense of humiliation grows deeper as a result of these actions and enflames the existing feelings of hatred and anger that creates a climate that breeds violence—violence

26. See Hillesum, *Letters*.

that in turn heightens Israelis' sense of fear that provokes actions that deepen the Palestinian sense of humiliation, and on and on.[27]

Approaching the other to understand the other is an act of true love. It's the first step to take in order to love one's enemy and do good to those who harm one.

Loving the enemy does not prevent one from doing what is possible to save one's own life or country. But in saving oneself and one's country, one should still pray for those who persecute one, for God makes the sun rise on the evil and on the good and sends rain on the just and on the unjust.

This is the path that Jesus took to build the kingdom of God on earth. It is the path I want to take with like-minded people to promote the reign of God on earth.

I HAD A DREAM

The night I finished this chapter, I had a dream. In my dream I was in Bethsaida near the shore of the Sea of Galilee. As I was walking along a stream, which had its source in the Golan Heights and was winding its way through a wooded area to the Sea of Galilee, I saw a man sitting on a bench stroking a gazelle. Something about him attracted my attention. He was wearing a *kippah* and *tzitzit*. As I drew closer to him the gazelle trotted off. Spontaneously I called out, "Are you Jesus of Nazareth?" "Yes," he replied.

"Oh, Jesus, it's you. Can I talk to you? I have three major questions for you." He smiled and pointed to a place for me to sit beside him. I sat down. He didn't say anything. He seemed to be waiting for me to speak. So nervously I said, "In this chapter, I wrote about your mother. I want to know your response to what I wrote. My intentions were to honor your mother and you, though readers may think otherwise. I presented your mother as a phoenix that rose from the ashes of defilement. Since writing it, I imagine your mother crossing her arms over her body, where you are being formed, praising God in these words:

27. Goodman, *Catch-67*, 7–8.

> My soul magnifies the Lord,
> and my spirit rejoices in God my Savior,
> for he has looked with favor on the lowliness of his ser-
> vant. Surely, from now on all generations will call me
> blessed; for the Mighty One has done great things for me,
> and holy is his name. (Luke 1:46–49)

And when I think of you in her womb, I imagine you, despite the violence of your origins, addressing God in these words:

> For it was you who formed my inward parts;
> you knit me together in my mother's womb.
> I praise you, for I am fearfully and wonderfully made.
> Wonderful are your works. (Ps 139:13–17)

Jesus looked at me compassionately and asked, "How do you think I would respond to such a happening? If I had met a fifteen-year-old girl who had been brutally raped and became pregnant, do you think I would look down on her? Would she not evoke my compassion and respect for her and her child! Or would she and her child be debased in my eyes? My mother was a warrior woman who had the courage to rise up out of humiliating conditions."

"Oh, Jesus, I know what you would do. When you were on earth you proclaimed God's love for all people as well as God's special love for those who were debased and marginalized."

We both sat quietly for a time, and then I said, "This is my second question. Did you ordain twelve apostles at the Last Supper and make known that you intended that only men could be priests?" Jesus turned to me and said, "Why are you asking me that question when you know the answer. You know I was a Jew and remained a Jew. You know that I did not found a church. After I died my disciples met in memory of me, and remained faithful Jews. When more and more gentiles entered the church, the church gradually parted from Judaism and formed itself into a royal kingdom governed by princes wearing miters and toting staffs. That, thank God, is now gradually changing."

Then, without pausing, I gave my third statement. "In the horrors of the Holocaust, you were, so to speak, crucified again and again with the extermination of your Jewish brothers and sisters.

I say this, because a gentile church, beginning with the writings of Paul and the Gospel writers, pitted the Jews against you."

Jesus began to weep. Between his sobs, he said, "Something went wrong in the beginning with the severing of relations between Jews and Christians. The road taken, the road of supersessionism, was a road to death. My followers became heirs to traditions that demonized the Jews."

I looked at Jesus. His face was so filled with sadness. I, too, began to cry. After several moments of silence, Jesus said, "The church needs to revise its teachings on me."

The alarm went off. I woke up. I was back in this world.

Chapter 7

Who Is God for Me?

God is not transcendent, mysterious and inapproachable, but my immediate companion. I live in God and experience God in God's full immediacy.

–Joseph Soloveitchik[1]

GOD TALKS TO ME

The theme of the Bible is God's encounter with us humans. Either openly or by implication the biblical stories are reports of encounters with God.

Na'aseh ve-nishma, "We will do and we will hear," are among the most famous words in Judaism. They are what the Israelites said when they accepted the covenant at Sinai (Exod 24:3). In Deut 5:27 the verbs are reversed, *shmanu ve-asehnu*, "We will hear and we will do."

1. Soloveitchik, *Halakhic Man*, #.

"*We will hear and we will do*" declares a readiness to hear God speaking to us in the Now. Life itself is the living Scripture. We experience what God wants of us in this hour, in what has now approached us—and it demands our response. I give my answer by accomplishing among the options available that which seems to me to be the next right step, though proof is found in the results.

In chapter 2, I examined how our biblical ancestors heard God speaking to them and their responses. Eve heard God talking to her through a serpent (I believe she did); Abraham heard God talking to him through his dissatisfaction with life (his wife was barren and all around him felt barren); Tamar was faced with a decision she had to make, either do something to solve a problem or do nothing and leave the rest to chance; and Moses heard God speaking to him in what seemed to be a bush on fire (Moses questioned God's commands); in all these cases, including the questionable response of Tamar, history proved that they had taken the next right step.

God spoke to me in similar fashion. Curiosity about Jesus drove me to Israel. Accounts by Jews of the church's relationship to them throughout history led me to study the history of the church with the Jews. The Nazi liquidation of Jews in Christian Europe convinced me that if the church ignored this event, its very existence would need to be questioned. In view of such atrocious Christian treatment of Jews, I asked myself if it would not have been better if Jesus had not been born. As I continued to study, I came to be convinced that such atrocities were possible only through a profound abuse of Jesus' name and message.

When I look at where I am now in writing this book, I sense how God spoke to me through my curiosity, my questions, the horror I experienced, and the decisions I made. In walking this road, God was my companion, and dare I say that we became lovers!

FALLING IN LOVE WITH GOD

In Deut 6:5 it is written, "You shall love the LORD your God with all your heart, and with all your soul, and with all your might." That sounds like a command to fall in love with God. But how is that expressed? Can I express my love for God directly and immediately, or is my love for God expressed only indirectly by what I do?

That question was hotly debated from ancient times between two schools of thought: that of Rabbi Akiva and Rabbi Ishmael (both of whom lived shortly before and after the destruction of the temple in 70 CE).

The school of Rabbi Ishmael claimed that a direct encounter with God was impossible. How, the rabbi asked, can one approach God who is a "consuming fire" (Exod 24:17) and whose throne is "fiery flames" (Dan 7:9)? The distance between God and the person can only be bridged indirectly through "sacred places and sacred times, sacred liturgy and sacred ritual, sacred writings and sacred individuals (priest and lawgiver, prophet and sage)."[2] To "hold fast [cleave] to God" (Deut 30:20) is by way of mediators—learning from sages how to walk in God's ways, . . . The Holy and Blessed One said, "If you fulfill my commandments you will become like Me."

The school of Rabbi Akiva argued for a direct relationship with God, which he saw contained in the command "You shall love the LORD your God with all your heart, and with all your soul, and with all your might." The command is given directly to "you" in the singular. *You* shall love the Lord your God with all *your* heart, and with all *your* soul, and with all *your* might. No question of a mediator is implied. For Akiva the created world was invested with divinity; the earth is heaven and earth together. A continuous permeable flow passes continually between the two. Direct encounter with God has taken place since the beginning of time.[3]

But a remark of Jesus, in the Gospel according to John, puts direct encounter with God in question: "I am the way, and the truth, and the life. No one comes to the Father except through me" (14:6). James Dunn, a well-known New Testament scholar, summarized this tradition in the following words:

2. Dunn, *Did the First Christians*, 149–50.

3. For an extended discussion of this topic see Heschel, *Heavenly Torah*, ch. 10, "Duties of the Heart," 189–207.

Christian reflection on the significance and status of Jesus has been Christianity's principal attempt to make sense of how the gulf between the divine and the human is to be crossed. All religions are in their own ways attempts to affirm that the infinite gulf between Creator and creation can be bridged and to show how that bridging takes place. In each case sacred places and sacred times, sacred liturgy and sacred ritual, sacred writings and sacred individuals (priest and lawgiver, prophet and sage), play critical roles. But Christianity has gone a step further in declaring that God has bridged the gulf not merely in scripture and temple, not only through priest and prophet, but in a particular individual (Jesus) through whom God revealed himself and who constitutes the bridge over the gulf in himself.[4]

Geza Vermes, the New Testament historian, counters with a different position.

In the Synoptic Gospels, unlike in the rest of the New Testament, the focal point of reflection and teaching is God, and not Jesus or Christ. It is towards God, the heavenly Father, that prayers and worship are directed without mediators. It is the Father himself who listens to supplications, offers a helping hand, and acts as protection, comforter and savior. Surrounded by an aura of charisma, the religion practiced and preached by Jesus was meant to be a passport allowing the holder without let or hindrance and without the need for other go-betweens to enter directly into the Kingdom of God. Christocentricity does not stem from the historical Jesus.[5]

In the Synoptic Gospels, direct encounter with God is possible. Jesus taught his followers to address God as Father: "Pray then like this: 'Our Father in heaven, hallowed be your name'" (Matt 6:9). The relationship between parent and child is direct. If one can have a direct relationship with God, are emotions involved?

4. Dunn, *Did the First Christians*, 149–50.
5. Vermes, *Jesus the Jew*, 60.

The Rambam (also known as Maimonides), the foremost intellectual figure of medieval Judaism (1145–1204), wrote,

> What is the proper [degree] of love? (It is) that a person should love God with a very great and exceeding love until his soul is bound up in the love of God. Thus, he will always be obsessed with this love as if he is lovesick. [A lovesick person's] thoughts are never diverted from the love of that woman. He is always obsessed with her; when he sits down, when he gets up, when he eats and drinks. With an even greater [love], the love for God should be [implanted] in the hearts of those who love Him and are obsessed with Him at all times as we are commanded, "love the LORD your God with all your heart and with all your soul and with all your might" (Deut 6:5).[6]

What the Rambam has written may sound exaggerated. But similar descriptions are found in the psalms; e.g., in Ps 63, the psalmist begins by addressing God as "O God, you are *my* God" and then exclaims, "Earnestly I seek you; my soul thirsts for you; my flesh faints for you, as in a dry and weary land where there is no water." And then he adds, "My soul clings to you; your right hand upholds me."

In Hos 2, Israel is referred to as God's unfaithful wife. God, unable to let her go, seeks her:

> Therefore, I will hedge up her way with thorns, and I will build a wall against her, so that she cannot find her paths. . . .
>
> Then she shall say, "I will go and return to my first husband, for it was better for me then than now." . . .
>
> Therefore, I will now allure her and bring her into the wilderness and speak tenderly to her. . . .
>
> There she shall answer as in the days of her youth, . . . on that day [she] will call me "My Husband," and no longer will [she] call me "My Baal." (Hos 2:6–7, 14–16)

And when she does return, God says,

---

6. Maimonides, *Mishneh Torah, Hilkhot Teshuva*, 10:3.

> And I will betroth you to me forever. I will betroth you to
> me in righteousness and in justice, in steadfast love and
> in mercy. I will betroth you to me in faithfulness. And
> you shall know the Lord. (Hos 2:19–20)

Every morning Jews wrap the leather strap of the tefillin (phylacteries—black leather boxes containing Torah readings inscribed on tiny scrolls of parchment that are strapped onto the arms and forehead) around their ring finger, and say,

> And I will betroth you to me forever. I will betroth you to
> me in righteousness and in justice, in steadfast love and
> in mercy. I will betroth you to me in faithfulness. And
> you shall know the Lord.

But they do not wear tefillin on the Sabbath.

The Sabbath and Betrothal

The Sabbath in Judaism replaces the putting on of tefillin as an expression of one's betrothal to God. On the Sabbath, the synagogue service begins with the words, "I am my beloved's and my beloved is mine" (Song 2:16). This is followed by the hymn "Yedid Nefesh": "O most dearly beloved! O merciful One! Draw me . . . O most splendid! O light of the world! My soul is love-sick because of You."[7]

But the Sabbath, as an expression of betrothal, doesn't belong solely to Israel. The Sabbath was given to the whole of humanity at creation: "God blessed the seventh day and made it holy, because on it God rested from all his work that he had done in creation" (Gen 2:3). Since then, we, too, have been invited to observe the Sabbath:

> Remember the Sabbath day, to keep it holy. Six days you
> shall labor, and do all your work, but the seventh day is
> a Sabbath to the Lord your God. On it you shall not do
> any work . . . For in six days the Lord made heaven and
> earth, the sea, and all that is in them, and rested on the

7. *Service of the Heart*, 5.

seventh day. Therefore, the LORD blessed the Sabbath day
and made it holy. (Exod 20:8–11)

In imitation of God, Jesus observed the Sabbath: When he came to Nazareth, where he had been brought up, he went to the synagogue on the Sabbath day, *as was his custom* (Luke 4:16). Jesus' followers continued to observe the Sabbath after his death. Joseph of Arimathea took Jesus' body from the cross, "wrapped it in a linen shroud and laid it in a tomb cut in stone. . . . It was the Day of Preparation, and the Sabbath was beginning. . . . On the Sabbath they rested according to the commandment . . . But on the first day of the week, at early dawn, they went to the tomb, taking the spices they had prepared" (Luke 23:54—24:1). In my love for God, I observe the sabbath in imitation of Jesus.

Teshuvah/Repentance: Mending Relationships

Like the woman in the book of Hosea, we all have moments when we drift away from God and our own deeper selves. God comes seeking us, in different manners, like a parent who punishes a child and like a lover luring a beloved. When we do return there is great rejoicing. And like the unfaithful woman, who redoubled her efforts to prove her love for her husband, we, too, want to make up for our infidelity.

I know from experience that this can be done. At a number of meetings, I argued with a person I found most unattractive. Then I said something that truly debased her in the eyes of others. I was shocked at what I said. An apology wasn't sufficient. To help make up, I invited her to dinner at a special restaurant. That act, and other acts of mine, and her responses to me, developed into a deep and lasting friendship.

From this experience I gained a new understanding of two quotations, one from the Talmud and the other from the New Testament:

In the place where repentant sinners stand, even the
wholly righteous cannot stand. (Ber. 34b)

> Just so, I tell you, there will be more joy in heaven over
> one sinner who repents than over ninety-nine righteous
> persons who need no repentance. (Luke 15:7)

While I still regret how nasty I was, I am also grateful for it. Without that moment we probably would never have become such close friends.

Repairing the damage one has inflicted on another is one of the steps in repentance. The word "repentance" is a word translated from the Hebrew word *teshuvah*, which literally means getting back on track. It is considered to be one of the seven gifts given by God at creation.

Teshuvah, repentance, is connected to free will, which is the ability to repair and create oneself. *Teshuvah* has no relationship with washing one's sins away. Sin, though forgiven, remains etched in our being, and can be a source of energy to go forward:

> There is a past that persists in its existence that does not
> vanish and disappear but remains firm in its place. Such
> a past enters into the domain of the present, and links
> up with the future. . . . Both—past and future—are alive;
> both act and create in the heart of the present and shape
> the very image of reality. From this perspective we nei-
> ther perceive the past as "no more" nor the future as "not
> yet" nor the present as a "fleeting moment." Rather, past,
> present, future merges and blends together, and this new
> three-fold time structure arises before us adorned with a
> splendid unity. The past is joined to the future, and both
> are reflected in the present.[8]

Memory is important. Remembered sins become spiritual springboards for increased inspiration and evaluation:

> Compared to those for whom repentance is a wholly
> miraculous phenomenon made possible by the endless
> grace of the Almighty, Judaism does not indulge in weep-
> ing and despair, does not lacerate his flesh or flail away at
> himself. He does not afflict himself with penitential rites

8. Soloveitchik, *Halakhic Man*, 114.

and forgoes all mortification of body and soul. Halakhic man is engaged in self-creation, in creating a new "I." He does not regret an irretrievably lost past but a past still in existence, one that stretches into and interpenetrates with the present and the future.[9]

The creation of a new self is visible in the life of Jacob (Gen 25–34). Jacob is the twin brother of Esau, who was the firstborn. Both are sons of Isaac and Rebecca.

We are not told a lot about Esau. Jacob is the hero of this story, which doesn't mean that he was perfect. He was named Jacob at his birth, a name that is often interpreted as someone who seizes and supplants (Gen 27:36). One day Esau, exhausted and starving, found Jacob with a pot of stew that he had just cooked. He begged, "Let me eat some of that red stew, for I am exhausted!" Jacob said, "Sell me your birthright now." Esau said, "I am about to die; of what use is a birthright to me?" Jacob continued, "Swear to me now." So he swore to him and sold his birthright to Jacob. Jacob gave Esau bread and lentil stew.

Sometime after this episode, Jacob took advantage of his father's age and blindness and stole the blessing reserved for Esau, the firstborn. Dressed as Esau, he entered his father's presence and said, "I am Esau your firstborn. I have done as you told me; now sit up and eat of my game, that your soul may bless me."

And Isaac blessed him:

> Let peoples serve you,
> and nations bow down to you.
> Be lord over your brothers,
> and may your mother's sons bow down to you.
> Cursed be everyone who curses you,
> and blessed be everyone who blesses you! (Gen 27:28–29)

When Esau discovered that Jacob had stolen his blessing, he decided to kill him. Terrified, Jacob fled with nothing except his staff (Gen 32:10). When he arrived in Haran he worked for Laban, his

---

9. Soloveitchik, "Sacred and Profane," 75–76.

mother's brother for a period of twenty or more years (Gen 31). When life became unbearable for him, he decided to return home.

When he neared Canaan, he sent messengers before him to Esau, instructing them to say to Esau, "I have sojourned with Laban and stayed until now. I have oxen, donkeys, flocks, male servants, and female servants. I have sent to tell my lord, in order that I may find favor in your sight.'" (Gen 32:3)

The messengers returned to Jacob with the news that Esau was on his way to meet him with four hundred men (Gen 32). Terrified, Jacob prayed, "Please deliver me from the hand of my brother, from the hand of Esau, for I fear him, that he may come and attack me, the mothers with the children" (Gen 32:9–11).

After his prayer, Jacob chose two hundred female goats and twenty male goats, two hundred ewes and twenty rams, thirty milking camels and their calves, forty cows and ten bulls, twenty female donkeys and ten male donkeys and said to his servants, "Pass on ahead of me and put a space between drove and drove. When Esau my brother meets you and asks you, 'To whom do you belong? Where are you going? And whose are these ahead of you?' then you shall say, 'They belong to your servant Jacob. They are a present sent to my lord Esau. And moreover, he is behind us'" (Gen 32:14–18).

What has happened? This is a changed scene. When Isaac blessed Jacob, Isaac said, "Be lord over your brothers and may your mother's sons bow down to you." Here, Jacob is bowing down to Esau.

After sending his family across the ford of the Jabbok, Jacob, alone by himself, had an encounter with a "man" (Gen 32:24). Many commentators have tried to explain the phrase "a man" wrestled with Jacob. In Hosea (12:4) the prophet states specifically that Jacob strove with an angel and prevailed. In this text, the mysterious being that appears suddenly as Jacob's adversary is described only as an *ish*, translated here as "a man." The *ish* could be himself. Even though scholars argue about who it was that Jacob was wrestling with, we do know that Jacob emerges from the struggle a new man. No longer will he be called Jacob, the supplanter, but *Israel,* embedded in which is God's name El, Isra-el. As Jacob departs from Esau, he says, "For I have seen your face, which is like seeing the face of God, and you have accepted me" (Gen 33:10).

Jacob, through repentance, is no longer Jacob, the supplanter, but Israel, a man of God. Repentance is my sure way back to God when I have sinned.

IN SUMMARY: GOD AND ME

In this chapter, I described my relationship with God in three inclusive terms: betrothal, the Sabbath, and *teshuvah.*

My concept of betrothal to God is modeled on Israel's betrothal to God, where God said,

> And I will take you for my wife forever; I will take you for
> my wife in righteousness and in justice, in steadfast love,
> and in mercy. I will take you for my wife in faithfulness;
> and you shall know the LORD. (Hos 2:19–20)

Such a teaching sounds like a huge exaggeration but not if we recall what I wrote above in chapter 6—that we are "endowed from birth with a divine soul," which "is bound and at one with its Source."[10] "The presence of God and the human person are so intermingled that in one way or another both remain indestructible and interdependent, (although) the very obscurity of the presence of each in the other means that they can appear to be separated."[11]

With such close proximity, conversation with God comes naturally:

> He it is, the innermost one,
> who awakens my being with his deep hidden touches.
>
> He it is who puts his enchantment upon these eyes
> and joyfully plays on the chords of my heart
> in varied cadence of pleasure and pain.

10. Jacobs, *On Ecstasy,* 63-67.

11. Rahner, "Concerning the Relationship," 234.

He it is who weaves the web of this maya
in evanescent hues of gold and silver, blue and green,
and lets peep out through the folds his feet,
at whose touch I forget myself.

Days come and ages pass,
and it is ever he who moves my heart in many a name,
in many a guise, in many a rapture of joy and of sorrow.[12]

On the Sabbath, the tefillin are not worn. Observance of the Sabbath expresses betrothal. The Song of Songs has a special place in the Sabbath liturgy. Most of the words in the Song express intertwining words of lovers.[13]

O that his left hand were under my head,
and that his right hand embraced me! (2:6)

You are altogether beautiful, my love;
there is no flaw in you. (4:7)

I am my beloved's and my beloved is mine. (6:3)

You are a garden fountain,
A well of living water,
and flowing streams from Lebanon. (4:15)

There was controversy about admitting the Song to the canon. Rabbi Akiva (d. 135 CE), who read the Song allegorically, insisted that there had never been any doubt about its canonical status:

God forbid! No man in Israel ever disputed the status of the Song of Songs . . . for the whole world is not worth the day on which the Song of Songs was given to Israel; for all the writings are holy, but the Song of Songs is the holiest of the holy.[14]

12. Tagore, *Gitanjali*, 133.

13. The words in italics are the woman's and the words in regular style are the man's.

14. Mishnah, Yad. 3:5.

Teshuvah is the gift God gave us to transform the straw of our lives into gold. The example I gave of such transformation is Jacob. By means of *teshuvah*, Jacob had a name change, from Jacob, the supplanter, to Israel (Isra-El), a name in which God's name is embedded. To repeat, the transformative power of *teshuvah* is expressed in these words:

> In the place where repentant sinners stand, even the wholly righteous cannot stand. (Ber. 34b)

> Just so, I tell you, there will be more joy in heaven over one sinner who repents than over ninety-nine righteous persons who need no repentance. (Luke 15:7)

The power of *teshuvah* is the ability to mend one's relationship with God, with others, and with oneself, despite how low one has fallen.

But *teshuvah* is not a magical gift where sins are forgiven and washed away. Instead, the onus of responsibility rests on the sinner, to recognize one's sins, regret them to the extent that one is able, and set out to repair them. It is this process that gives joy, not only in heaven but to oneself. Chains are broken, burdens uplifted, and eyes opened to a world teeming with life.

These three gifts have nourished and strengthened my relationship with God and with others. Through them the world has become God-real for me. I want never to forget that noblesse oblige. I pray to have ears that hear and eyes that see, in fulfillment of the words, "We will hear and we will do" (Deut 5:27).

So, I conclude,

> God, my beloved, help me become mindful of others and attuned to you. You, who are . . . not transcendent, mysterious and inapproachable, but my immediate Companion. I live in You and experience You in Your full immediacy.[15]

---

15. Adapted from Sloveitchik, "Sacred and Profane," 63 (I've changed the word "God" to "You").

Looking Ahead

Phoenix drawing made in ash.

To move from a traditional stance of "superiority over" to one of "authentic dialogue with" requires a pluralistic Christology that renews Jesus' focus on the reign of God rather than on the reign of the church and that understands Jesus as "a way that is open to other ways."

For me, Jesus belongs to everyone; he is one with everyone, but he especially belongs to misfits, whoever they are. Though a faithful Jew, Jesus was set apart in an uncomfortably conspicuous way. To know him as a historical human being is to know that the most humiliated of us can rise from the ashes like a phoenix.

And as we rise from the ashes, as he did, we will turn with care and concern to sinners and misfits.

Jesus is remembered for encouraging us to use the gift of repentance (toward the abuser and the self) for the creation of one's authentic self, a self who belongs and is one with everyone. The gift of repentance is the gift par excellence to mend broken relationships among individuals and among nations.

Among the plurality of Christologies in the New Testament[1] and the multiple Christologies that have arisen since the 1950s[2] is the Christology in this book—Jesus as truly divine and truly human, with all the gifts and weaknesses that are the lot of humans. He came to be one with everyone, not to lord it over anyone.

He belongs to everyone, as we believe the Buddha, for example, belongs to everyone. In a pluralistic Christology, Jesus takes his place among the many religious leaders and enlightened beings. But it is a special, indeed a distinctive or unique place. While each religious figure from the various traditions is distinct or unique in their own way, Jesus' distinctiveness is to be found in his particular and radical call to love not just our friends, not just our neighbors, but also our enemies. He called his followers to love their enemies and to pray for those who persecuted them, in imitation of the God who makes the sun rise on the evil and the good and sends rain on the just and on the unjust (Matt 5:44–45). Such a love of enemies did not, however, prevent Jesus from opposing their policies and actions. But that opposition was motivated by a love for his oppressors/enemies that was as great as his love for the oppressed.

Only with such a universal love, embracing friend and enemies, can our world of discord and injustice truly be changed— only so can the world, and Jesus' name, be redeemed.

1. Haight, *Jesus*, 152–84.
2. Johnson, *Consider Jesus*.

Bibliography

Avila, Theresa. "The Interior Castle." In *The Complete Works of Saint Theresa of Jesus*, 2:187–351. London: Sheed & Ward, 1946.

Allen, Elise Ann. "Vatican Cardinal Tries to Heal Rift with Jews after Pope's Rhetoric on Torah." *Crux*, September 13, 2021. https://cruxnow.com/vatican/2021/09/vatican-cardinal-tries-to-heal-rift-with-jews-after-popes-rhetoric-on-torah.

Allen, John L. Jr. "Pope Gets Lucky as Trip Offers Unplanned Chance to Reassure Jews." *Crux*, September 14, 2021. https://cruxnow.com/news-analysis/2021/09/pope-gets-lucky-as-trip-offers-unplanned-chance-to-reassure-jews.

Allen, Woody, dir. *Crimes and Misdemeanors*. 1989; Los Angeles: Orion Pictures.

Barrows, Anita, and Joanna Macy, trans. *Rilke's Book of Hours*. New York: Riverside, 1996.

Buber, Martin. *Between Man and Man*. London: Kegan Paul, 1947.

———. *I and Thou*. Translated by Walter Kaufmann. New York: Simon & Schuster, 1970.

———. *On the Bible: Eighteen Studies*. New York: Schocken, 1982.

———. *Two Types of Faith*. Translated by Norman Goldhawk. London: Routledge & Kegan Paul, 1951.

Brown, Raymond. *The Birth of the Messiah*. New York: Doubleday, 1977.

———. *The Gospel According to John*. New York: Doubleday, 1966.

———. *An Introduction to the New Testament*. New York: Doubleday, 1997.

Chabad. "Human Potential." https://www.chabad.org/library/article_cdo/aid/1184/jewish/Human-Potential.htm.

Chavel, Charles B. "The Releasing of a Prisoner on the Eve of Passover in Ancient Jerusalem." *Journal of Biblical Literature* 60:3 (Sep 1941) 273–78.

Chrysostom, John. *Eight Homilies against the Jews*. Glasgow: Good Press, 2010. Kindle ed.

Cohen, Gershon. "The Talmudic Age." In *Study Guide to Great Ages and Ideas of the Jewish People*, 143–211. Jerusalem: Hadassah Education Department, 1958.

Cohen, Jeremy. *Christ Killers: The Jews and the Passion from the Bible to the Big Screen*. Oxford: Oxford University Press, 2007.

Cook, Michael. *Modern Jews Engage the New Testament: Jewish Well-Being in a Christian Environment.* Woodstock, VT: Jewish Lights, 2008.

Cunningham, Philip A. *Jesus and the Evangelists.* Lanham, MD: University Press of America, 1993.

Demann, Paul. "La Catéchèse Chrétienne et le Peuple de la Bible. Constations et Perspectives." *Cahiers Sioniens* 3–4 (1952) 23–25.

Deutsch, Celia. "Journey to Dialogue: Sisters of Our Lady of Sion and the Writing of Nostra Aetate." *SCJR* 11:1 (2016) 1–36.

Donin, Hayim Halevy. *To Pray as a Jew.* New York: Basic, 1980.

Duffy, Eamon. *Madonnas That Maim? Christianity and the Cult of the Virgin.* UK: Blackfriars, 1999.

Dunn, James. *Did the First Christians Worship Jesus?* Louisville: John Knox, 2010.

———. *Jesus, Paul, and the Gospels.* Grand Rapids: Eerdmans, 2011.

Encyclopaedia Judaica. Jerusalem: Keter, 1972.

Fishbane, Michael. *Sacred Attunement: A Jewish Theology.* Chicago: University of Chicago Press, 2008.

Flannery, Edward. *The Anguish of the Jews: Twenty-Three Centuries of Anti-Semitism.* London: Macmillan, 1965.

Fleischner, Eva, ed. *Auschwitz: Beginning of a New Era? Reflections on the Holocaust.* Jersey City: Ktav, 1977.

Flusser, David. *Jesus.* Jerusalem: Magnus, 1998.

Francis. "General Audience." Rome, Italy, August 11, 2021. https://www.youtube.com/watch?v=9BiDP4SR9SY.

Frankl, Viktor E. *Man's Search for Meaning.* Boston: Beacon, 2006.

Fredriksen, Paula, and Adele Reinhartz, eds. *Jesus, Judaism, and Christian Anti-Judaism: Reading the New Testament after the Holocaust.* Louisville: Westminster John Knox, 2002.

Fritz, Maureena. "Revelation and Self-Understanding: A Comparative Study of Gabriel Moran and Carl Roger." University of Ottawa: Ottawa, 1971.

Goodman, Micah. *Catch-67: The Left, the Right, and the Legacy of the Six-Day War.* Translated by Eylon Levy. London: Yale University Press, 2018.

Green, Arthur. *Seek My Face: A Jewish Mystical Theology.* Woodstock, VT: Jewish Lights, 2003.

Greenberg, Irving. "Cloud of Smoke, Pillar of Fire: Judaism, Christianity and Modernity after the Holocaust." In *Auschwitz: Beginning of a New Era? Reflections on the Holocaust,* edited by Eva Fleischner, 7–55. New York: Ktav, 1977.

Haight, Roger. *Jesus, Symbol of God.* New York: Orbis, 1999.

Heschel, Abraham Joshua. *Heavenly Torah: As Refracted through the Generations.* Edited and translated by Gordon Tucker. New York: Continuum, 2010.

Hilberg, Raul. *The Destruction of the European Jews.* New Haven: Yale University Press, 1961.

Hill, Brennan, et al. *Faith, Religion, and Theology: A Contemporary Introduction.* Mystic, CT: Twenty-Third, 1989.

Hillesum, Etty. *Letters from Westerbork.* New York: Pantheon, 1986.

Isaac, Jules. *Jesus and Israel.* Translated by Sally Gran. New York: Holt, Rinehart and Winston, 1971.

Jacobs, Louis, trans. and ed. *On Ecstasy: A Tractate by Dobh Baer of Lubavitch.* New York: Rossel, 1963.

John Paul II. *Ordinatio Sacerdotalis.* Vatican City: Libreria Editrice Vaticana, 1994.

———. *We Remember: A Reflection on the Shoah.* Rome: Vatican Council, 1998.

Johnson, Elizabeth A. *Consider Jesus: Waves of Renewal in Christology.* UK: Chapman, 1990.

Josephus, Flavius. *The New Complete Works of Josephus.* Translated by William Whiston. Grand Rapids: Kregel, 1999.

Kasper, Cardinal Walter. "The Commission for Religious Relations with the Jews: A Crucial Endeavor of the Catholic Church." Presented at Boston College, November 6, 2002.

———. "The Relationship of the Old and the New Covenant as One of the Central Issues in Jewish-Christian Dialogue." Presented at the Centre for the Study of Jewish-Christian Relations, Cambridge, UK, December 6, 2004.

Keenan, John. *Earthing the Cosmic Christ of Ephesians: The Universe, the Trinity, and Zhiyi's Threefold Truth 1.* Eugene, OR: Wipf and Stock, 2021.

Kessler, Edward. "A Jewish Response to Hans Hermann Henrix and Barbara Meyer." In *Christ Jesus and the Jewish People Today: New Explorations of Theological Interrelationships,* written by Philip A. Cunningham et al, 157–63. Grand Rapids: Eerdmans, 2011.

Klausner, Joseph. *Jesus of Nazareth: His Life, Times, and Teaching.* New York: Macmillan, 1925.

Knitter, Paul F. "Christianity and the Religions: A Zero-Sum Game? Reclaiming the Path Not Taken and the Legacy of Krister Stendahl." *JES* 46 (Winter 2011) 5–21.

———. *Jesus and the Other Names.* New York: Orbis, 1996.

———. *One Earth Many Religions.* New York: Orbis, 1995.

Kugel, James L. *The Bible as It Was.* Cambridge, MA: Belknap, 1997.

Levine, Amy-Jill. *The Misunderstood Jew: The Church and the Scandal of the Jewish Jesus.* New York: HarperCollins, 2007.

Lewis, Charlton T., and Charles Short. *A Latin Dictionary.* New York: Nigel Wetters Gourlay, 2020.

Lichtenberg, Jean-Paul. *From the First to the Last of the Just.* Jerusalem: Ecumenical Theological Research Fraternity in Israel, 1979.

Lovelace, Richard. "To Althea, from Prison." *Poetry Foundation.* https://www.poetryfoundation.org/poems/44657/to-althea-from-prison.

Lumen Gentium: The Dogmatic Constituion on the Church. Vatican City, 1964.

Maimonides. *Avodah Zarah.* In *Shishah Sidrei Mishnah: The Mishnah; Seder Nezikin.* Vol. 4, *Avodah Zarah Pirkei Avot Horayot.* Translated by Roy Abramowitz. Jerusalem: Eliner Library, 1994.

Meier, John. *A Marginal Jew: Rethinking the Historical Jesus.* New York: Doubleday, 1991.

BIBLIOGRAPHY

The Merriam-Webster Dictionary. Springfield, MA: Merriam-Webster, 2019.

Newman, John Henry. "Discourse 7." *The Idea of a University*. Oxford: Oxford University Press, 1852.

Nostra Aetate: Declaration on the Relation of the Church to Non-Christian Religions. Vatican City, 1965.

Parkes, James. *The Conflict of the Church and Synagogue: A Study in the Origins of Anti-Semitism*. London: Soncino, 1934.

Philo. *On the Creation of the Cosmos According to Moses*. Philo of Alexandria Commentary 1. Translated by David T. Runia. Atlanta, GA: Society of Biblical Literature, 2005.

Pius X, Statement in his meeting with Theodor Herzl, Jan. 25, 1904. See: https://jewinthepew.org/2015/01/25/25-january-1904-pope-pius-x-gives-theodor-herzls-zionist-project-a-cold-reception-otdimjh-onthisday/

Pius XII. *Munificentissimus Deus*. November 1, 1950. Vatican website. https://www.vatican.va/content/pius-xii/en/apost_constitutions/documents/hf_p-xii_apc_19501101_munificentissimus-deus.html.

Plus, Raoul. *God within Us*. New York: Kenedy and Sons, 1949.

The Pontifical Biblical Commission. *The Jewish People and Their Sacred Scriptures in the Christian Bible*. Rome: Libreria Editrice Vaticana, 2002.

Rahner, Karl. "Concerning the Relationship between Nature and Grace." In *Theological Investigations* 1 (1961) 156-65.

Schaberg, Jane. *The Illegitimacy of Jesus: A Feminist Theological Interpretation of the Infancy Narratives*. New York: Sheffield Phoenix, 2006.

Service of the Heart. Jerusalem: Kol Haneshama, 2007.

Soloveitchik, Joseph. *Halakhic Man*. Philadelphia: Jewish Publication Society, 1983.

————. "Sacred and Profane." *Jewish Thought* 3:1 (Fall/winter 1993) 55–82.

Stendahl, Krister. *Meanings: The Bible as Document and Guide*. Philadelphia: Fortress, 1984.

Tagore, Rabindranath. *Gitanjali*. New Delhi: Rajiv Beri for Macmillan India Limited, 1998.

Tillich, Paul. *Systematic Theology*. Vol. 1. Chicago: University of Chicago Press, 1951.

The Vatican Commission for Religious Relations with the Jews. *Guidelines and Suggestions for Implementing the Conciliar Declaration Nostra aetate*. Rome: Vatican City State, 1974.

————. *Notes on the Correct Way to Present Jews and Judaism in Preaching and Catechesis of the Roman Catholic Church*. Rome: Libreria Editrice Vaticana, 1985.

Vermes, Geza. *Christian Beginnings From Nazareth to Nicaea AD 30–35*. London: Penguin, 2012.

————. *Jesus the Jew: A Historian's Reading of the Gospels*. Philadelphia: Fortress, 1981.

Warner, Marina. *Alone of All Her Sex: The Myth and the Cult of the Virgin Mary*. New York: Vintage, 1983.

BIBLIOGRAPHY

Wiesel, Elie. *A Passover Haggadah*. New York: Simon & Schuster, 1993.
Zornberg, Avivah Gottlieb. *Genesis: The Beginning of Desire*. Philadelphia: Jewish
Publication Society, 1995.

www.ingramcontent.com/pod-product-compliance
Lightning Source LLC
Chambersburg PA
CBHW070740030726